▶ もう少し詳しく：Listening Section

Part 1： 写真の内容は「人（1人または複数）」、「物」、「風景」、あるいはこれらを組み合わせたもの。選択肢は、現在進行形で「人が何かをしている」や、〈be 「物がどこに／どういう状態である」などの描写文がありま

Part 2： 質問にはW/H疑問文、Yes/No疑問文、選択疑問文（A による発言もあります。応答には「直接応答」と「間接応答 に対してYou should ask at the police box.という応答）があります。

Part 3： 会話は男女2人によるものが中心で、3人（男性2人・女性1人または男性1人・女性2人）の会話もあります。また、会話に関係する図表が示され、それを参照して解答する問題も。会話の多くは「問題・要求→提案→結論」のように展開されます。設問には、「概要（話題、場所など）」、「詳細（問題、要求、提案、理由、発言者の意図、図表に関する情報など）」、「結論（次の行動、新たな提案など）を問うものが多くあります。

Part 4： トークの種類には、「電話メッセージ」、「会議の一部」、「お知らせ」、「放送」、「スピーチ」、「話（説明、お願い、指示）」などがあります。トークは概ね「挨拶→概要→詳細→結論」で展開し、設問はPart 3と同じ傾向で、図表が含まれるものもあります。

▶ もう少し詳しく：Reading Section

Part 5： 空所に当てはまる語彙、品詞、前置詞、動詞・助動詞、接続詞などを選択する問題で、文法力と語彙力が問われます。

Part 6： 1つの文書中に4つの空所があり、うち3つが語句による穴埋めで、残りの1つが文による穴埋めになっています。いずれの場合も、解答には前後を読み、文脈から判断する必要があります。

Part 7： 出題形式が3つあります。問題文が、①「1つの文書」のもの、②「2つの文書」のもの、③「3つの文書」のものです。②の場合、一方がEメールであることが多く、また③の場合、Eメールと図表が含まれる傾向があります。

▶Proficiency Scale: TOEIC® L&Rとコミュニケーション能力との相関表

レベル	TOEICスコア	評価(ガイドライン)
A	860	**Non-Nativeとして十分なコミュニケーションができる。** 自己の経験の範囲内では、専門外の分野の話題に対しても十分な理解とふさわしい表現ができる。Native Speakerの域には一歩隔たりがあるとはいえ、語彙・文法・構文のいずれをも正確に把握し、流暢に駆使する力を持っている。
B	730	**どんな状況でも適切なコミュニケーションができる素地を備えている。** 通常会話は完全に理解でき、応答もはやい。話題が特定分野にわたっても、対応できる力を持っている。業務上も大きな支障はない。正確さと流暢さに個人差があり、文法・構文上の誤りが見受けられる場合もあるが、意思疎通を妨げるほどではない。
C	430	**日常生活のニーズを充足し、** **限定された範囲内では業務上のコミュニケーションができる。** 通常会話であれば、要点を理解し、応答にも支障はない。複雑な場面における的確な対応や意思疎通になると、巧拙の差が見られる。 基本的な文法・構文は身についており、表現力の不足はあっても、ともかく自己の意思を伝える語彙を備えている。
D	220	**通常会話で最低限のコミュニケーションができる。** ゆっくり話してもらうか、繰り返しや言い換えをしてもらえば、簡単な会話は理解できる。 身近な話題であれば応答も可能である。 語彙・文法・構文ともに不十分なところは多いが、相手がNon-Nativeに特別な配慮をしてくれる場合には、意思疎通をはかることができる。
E		**コミュニケーションができるまでに至っていない。** 単純な会話をゆっくり話してもらっても、部分的にしか理解できない。 断片的に単語を並べる程度で、実質的な意思疎通の役には立たない。

一般財団法人 国際ビジネスコミュニケーション協会
https://www.iibc-global.org/library/default/toeic/official_data/lr/pdf/proficiency.pdf

▶TOEIC®テスト情報

TOEIC® L&Rをはじめ、TOEIC®のさまざまなテスト情報やデータなどが下のTOEIC®公式サイトより入手できます。

https://www.iibc-global.org/toeic.html
一般財団法人 国際ビジネスコミュニケーション協会 公式ページ

START WITH GRAMMAR REVIEW FOR THE TOEIC® L&R TEST

Contents

CHAPTER 1

基本文型

Shopping

本章での学習

▶文法：「基本文型(基本5文型)」と「There構文」の復習・確認
▶話題：Shopping
▶演習：Part 5 → Part 1 → Part 2 → Part 3 → Part 4形式の問題演習

事前学習

① Vocabulary 1とGrammar 1の問題に解答し、「語彙・文法クイズ」に備える。
② Part 3の音声を聞き、ディクテーション(書き取り)をする。

語彙・文法クイズ

Vocabulary 1とGrammar 1から5問(日本語→英語)

Vocabulary 1

Audio① 02

1～10の語句を英語にしましょう。その後で音声を聞いて確認しましょう。

1. 店員	___________ assistant
2. 店を経営する	___________ a store
3. このアプリを使う	use this ___________
4. 雇用	__________________
5. アンケート用紙に記入する	fill in a ____________________
6. 改装工事	________________ work
7. 一時的な店舗	________________ store
8. お詫びの印として	as a ___________ of apology
9. 不便を謝る	_______________ for inconvenience
10. ご迷惑をお掛けします。	Thank you for your ______________ .

Grammar 1

1 ～ 5の空所を埋めましょう。その後で、音声を聞いて確認しましょう。

1. 私は衣料品店でアルバイトをしています。
   I _________ part time at a clothing shop.

2. 彼女は買い物をしているときは楽しそうに見えます。
   She _________ happy when she is shopping.

3. 私は買い物があまり好きではない。
   I don't _________ shopping very much.

4. ジーンズを見せていただけますか。
   Could you _________ me some jeans?

5. その値段が私を驚かせた（私はその値段に驚いた）。
   The price _________ me surprised.

Pair Practice

・Vocabulary 1を、瞬時に「日本語→英語」にできるように、ペア（AとB）を組んで練習しましょう（1分間）。1分後にAとBの役割を交換し、同様に練習しましょう（1分間）。

A: 教科書を見ながらBに日本語を与える

B: 教科書を閉じたままAが与える日本語を英語にする

A: Bが即答できなければ、すぐにその英語を教え、1分間の内にどの語句もスラスラ英語で言えるようにさせる

・Grammar 1の例文についても同様の練習をしましょう（1分間）。

Grammar Review 1

基本文型

誰／何が（主語）＋ どうする（動詞）＋ ……………… ＋α（副詞）

英語の基本文型は、「誰／何が（主語）」＋「どうする（動詞）」で始まり、「どうする（動詞）」の意味によって後に続く語句が決まります（………の部分）。これによってできる文型を整理すると下のような5つの文型（基本5文型）にまとめられます。また、＋α（副詞：どのように、どこで、いつ、どうして）は必要に応じて、これらの文の後ろ（または文頭など）に加えられます。空所を埋めながら整理しましょう。

表の記号：S（主語）、V（動詞）、C（補語）、O（目的語）、α（副詞）

基本5文型	動　詞
1）第1文型: S + V + α I + __________ + α (in New York / for about a week). 私は、滞在した（ニューヨークに、約1週間）	自動詞（完全自動詞）
2）第2文型: S + V + C + α The restaurant + **is** + crowded + α (on weekends) そのレストランは、混んでいる（週末は）。 She + __________ + a singer + α (at the age of 16). 彼女は、なった、歌手に（16歳で）	自動詞（不完全自動詞） be, become, get, look, sound, feel, seem, keepなど
3）第3文型: S + V + O + α I + __________ + this book + α (online / last week). 私は、買った、この本を（オンラインで、先週）。	他動詞（完全他動詞）
4）第4文型: S + V + O_1（誰に）+ O_2（何を）+ α He + __________ + me + a call + α (late last night). 彼は、くれた、私に、電話を（遅くに、きのうの夜）。 I + **bought** + my father + a tie. 私は、買った、父に、ネクタイを。	他動詞（授与動詞） give, show, lend, get, bring, send, offer, leave, buy など
5）第5文型: S + V + O + C + α Their songs + __________ + me + happy. 彼らの歌は、させる、私を、ハッピーに。 My friends + **call** + me + Aki. 友人は、呼ぶ、私を、アキと。	他動詞（不完全他動詞） make, find, get, keep, leave, call など

■ There 構文：There is/are（ある／いる）+ S（何／誰が）+α（どこに）
表の基本5文型以外に「存在」を表す構文があります。S（何／誰が）が動詞の後に言われます。

____________ is	a book	on the desk.
あります、	一冊の本が、	机の上に
There ________	thirty students	in this English class.
いる、	30人の学生が、	この英語のクラスに

▶英語は語順が命

日本語には「は」「が」「を」「に」「の」といった格助詞があるため、下の①と②のように「ネコ」と「魚」の語順が入れ替わっても同じ内容を正しく伝えることができます。しかし、英語にはこうした格助詞がありません。代わりに語順が「〇〇が」「〇〇を」を示しています。したがって、③と④のようにcatとfishの位置が変わると意味も大きく変わってしまいます。

① ネコが 魚を 食べた。② 魚を ネコが 食べた。

③ A cat ate a fish.（ネコが／食べた／魚を） ④ A fish ate a cat.（魚が／食べた／ネコを）

▶C（補語）とは

補語とは文を成立させるために不足している意味を「補う語」です。第2文型と第5文型で使われます。

1) 第2文型：She (S) became (V) a singer (C).（彼女は／なった／歌手に）
この文は、She（彼女は）+ became（なった）で始まっています。これだけでは文が成立しません。「彼女は／なった」と言っているので、その後には「何に」（名詞）なったか、「どう」（形容詞）なったかを補う必要があります。この例文ではa singer（歌手）になったと名詞が補語になっています。もし、「有名に」なったのであればfamous（有名な）という形容詞を補語にして、She became famous.となります。

2) 第5文型：Their songs (S) make (V) me (O) happy (C).（彼らの歌は／する／私を／ハッピーに）
この文は、Their songs（彼らの歌が）+ make（する）+ me（私を）となっています。この後に、私を「何」（名詞）にするのか、私を「どう」（形容詞）するのかを補う語が必要です。この例文ではhappy（ハッピー）を補って、「私を」「ハッピーに」「する」と表現しています。

▶第 4 文型：S + V + O_1（誰に）+ O_2（何を）

第4文型は目的語を2つ持つ文型です。2つの目的がどのような語順になっているのか、少し詳しく見てみましょう。

1）英語では2つの目的語を並べる場合、「誰に」「何を」の語順を好みます。日本語はどうでしょう。「何を」が先で「誰に」が後になることが多いですね。このため注意が必要です。

2）ただ、英語でも「何を」を先に言いたいこともあります。その場合には次のようになります。

S　V　O_1　O_2 ➡	S　V　O_2 + to O_1	この形式になる動詞
誰に　何を He gave me a call.	何を　誰に He gave a call to me.	give, bring, lend, offer, pass, pay, send, show, teachなど
S　V　O_1　O_2 ➡	**S　V　O_2 + for O_1**	**この形式になる動詞**
誰に　何を I bought my father a tie.	何を　誰(のため)に I bought a tie for my father.	buy, make, get, cook, leaveなど

Exercises for the TOEIC® L&R Test

Part 5 Select the best answer to complete each sentence.

1. The sales assistant showed _______ a new model of the smartphone.
   (A) to me
   (B) for me
   (C) me
   (D) I

2. My mother and sister look very _______ when they are shopping.
   (A) to be happy
   (B) happy
   (C) happily
   (D) happiness

3. The shopping mall _______ open until 10 P.M. on weekdays.
   (A) is
   (B) are
   (C) becomes
   (D) makes

4. _______ is an information desk on the first floor at the entrance.
   (A) They
   (B) There
   (C) These
   (D) Those

5. This is a little too expensive. Could you _______ me a discount of one or two dollars?
   (A) find
   (B) pass
   (C) leave
   (D) give

Part 1 Listen and select the one statement that best describes what you see in the picture. **Audio① 04-06**

1.

Ⓐ Ⓑ Ⓒ Ⓓ

2.

Ⓐ Ⓑ Ⓒ Ⓓ

Part 2 Listen and select the best response to each question or statement. **Audio① 07-11**

1. Ⓐ Ⓑ Ⓒ 2. Ⓐ Ⓑ Ⓒ 3. Ⓐ Ⓑ Ⓒ 4. Ⓐ Ⓑ Ⓒ

Part 3 Listen and select the best answer to each question. **Audio① 12-14**

1. Where is this conversation taking place?
   (A) At a florist shop
   (B) At a jewelry store
   (C) At a cake shop
   (D) At a marriage agency

2. What occasion are they talking about?
   (A) A graduation
   (B) A birthday
   (C) A wedding
   (D) An employment

3. What does the man want to do?
   (A) To receive some flowers
   (B) To send some flowers
   (C) To fill in a questionnaire
   (D) To make a sample

Part 4 Listen and select the best answer to each question. Audio① 15-17

1. Where are you most likely to hear this announcement?
   (A) At a supermarket
   (B) At a hospital
   (C) At a station
   (D) At a library

2. What will happen to this place?
   (A) It will have a bargain sale.
   (B) It will have a new manager.
   (C) It will be closed for a few weeks.
   (D) It will stop business completely.

3. How much discount will customers get at the temporary store?
   (A) 10%
   (B) 12%
   (C) 15%
   (D) 20%

CHAPTER 2

名詞の修飾

At a Restaurant

本章での学習

▶文法：「名詞の修飾」の復習・確認
▶話題：At a Restaurant
▶演習：Part 5 → Part 6 → Part 7形式の問題演習

事前学習

① Vocabulary 2とGrammar 2の問題に解答し、「語彙・文法クイズ」に備える。
② Part 7の英文をチャンク単位で全文和訳をする。

語彙・文法クイズ

Vocabulary 1, 2とGrammar 1, 2から5問（日本語→英語）

Vocabulary 2

Audio① 18

1～10の語句を英語にしましょう。その後で音声を聞いて確認しましょう。

1.	多くの人を引き寄せる	＿＿＿＿＿＿ many people
2.	レストランレビュー（評価）	restaurant ＿＿＿＿＿＿
3.	スープに合う	go ＿＿＿＿＿ with the soup
4.	レストランの雰囲気	the ＿＿＿＿＿＿＿ of the restaurant
5.	メニューの品目	menu ＿＿＿＿＿
6.	カロリーを気にしている人たち	people ＿＿＿＿＿＿＿ about calories
7.	提供する	＿＿＿＿＿
8.	多種多様なオーガニック料理	a wide ＿＿＿＿＿＿ of organic dishes
9.	地元産の食材	locally ＿＿＿＿＿ ingredients
10.	サービス券を同封する	enclose a service ＿＿＿＿＿＿

Grammar 2

1 ～ 5の空所を埋めましょう。その後で、音声を聞いて確認しましょう。

1. フランスの人たちはワインが好きです。

   People ________ France like wine.

2. あそこでバスケットをやっている女の子たちは私のクラスメートです。

   The girls ____________ basketball over there are my classmates.

3. 日本語で書かれたメニューはありますか。

   Do you have a menu ____________ in Japanese?

4. 何か飲み物はいりますか。

   Do you want anything ______________ ?

5. 彼は去年イタリアから来たシェフです。

   He is the chef ________ came from Italy last year.

Pair Practice

・Vocabulary 2を、瞬時に「日本語→英語」にできるように、ペア（AとB）を組んで練習しましょう（1分間）。1分後にAとBの役割を交換し、同様に練習しましょう（1分間）。

A: 教科書を見ながらBに日本語を与える

B: 教科書を閉じたままAが与える日本語を英語にする

A: Bが即答できなければ、すぐにその英語を教え、1分間の内にどの語句もスラスラ英語で言えるようにさせる

・Grammar 2の例文についても同様の練習をしましょう（1分間）。

Grammar Review 2

名詞の修飾

「単独飾り」は名詞の前、「複合飾り」は名詞の後ろ

単独飾り ＋ 名詞
名詞 ＋ 複合飾り

英語で名詞を飾る（修飾する）ときの基本的なルールは、「単独飾り」（1語による修飾）は名詞の前、「複合飾り」（複数語による修飾）は名詞の後ろ、です。また、「飾り」の種類は、形容詞、前置詞句、現在分詞、過去分詞、to不定詞、関係詞節の全部で6タイプです。空所を埋めながら整理しましょう。

飾りの種類	例
1. 形容詞	＿＿＿＿ people 若い 人たち people **young at heart** 気持ちが若い人たち
2. 前置詞句	stress ＿＿＿＿ 仕事からの ストレス people **with a good sense of humor** ユーモアのセンスがよい 人たち
3. 現在分詞 ~ing （～している）	＿＿＿＿ people 働いている 人たち people **working in the IT business** IT業界で働いている 人たち
4. 過去分詞 （～された）	＿＿＿＿ foods 冷凍された 食品 pizza **frozen in the freezer** 冷凍庫で冷凍された ピザ
5. 不定詞 to ~ （～する）	a plan ＿＿＿＿ this summer この夏ハワイに行く 計画
6. 関係詞節 （関係代名詞、 関係副詞）	people ＿＿＿＿ **graduated from this university** この大学を卒業した 人たち the book (＿＿＿＿ **/that) our teacher recommended** 先生が薦めてくれた　本 the office ＿＿＿＿ **I work** 私が働く オフィス

▶名詞の後置修飾

私たちが英語で混乱する最大の要因は「語順」です。日本語とは大きく異なる「基本文型」(Grammar Review 1) の語順、そして、ここでの「名詞の修飾」の語順です。下の①は日本語と同じなので問題はないのですが、②のような「複合飾り」による後置修飾 (後ろからの修飾) が③のように文の中に含まれると、一気に文が難しく複雑に見えます。「基本文型」(Grammar Review 1) とこの「名詞の修飾」(Grammar Review 2) をしっかり理解しておくことで、④のように構造がつかめ、⑤の文と同じような感覚で容易に理解することができます。

① working people
働いている 人たち

② people working in the IT business
IT業界で働いている 人たち

③ People working in the IT business have a lot of stress from work.

④ People (working in the IT business) have a lot of stress (from work).
S: People / 後置修飾: (working in the IT business) / V: have / O: a lot of stress / 後置修飾: (from work)
人たち (IT業界で働いている) は 抱えている たくさんのストレス (仕事からの) を

⑤ People have stress.
S: People / V: have / O: stress

▶6種類の「飾り」

1) 形容詞

very youngなどは、youngをveryが強めているだけなので「複合飾り」とは考えません。なお、形容詞による「複合飾り」(後置修飾) はあまり見られません。

2) 前置詞句

前置詞は必ず名詞との組み合わせになるので、常に「複合飾り」(後置修飾) です。

3) 現在分詞

動詞にingを加えたもので、「〜している」と解釈しましょう。「単独飾り」にも「複合飾り」(後置修飾) にも使われます。

4) 過去分詞

動詞の3つ目の活用形（例：freeze, froze, frozen）で、「～された」と解釈しましょう。「単独飾り」にも「複合飾り」（後置修飾）にも使われます。

5) 不定詞

不定詞は、to + 動詞（原形）なので、常に「複合飾り」（後置修飾）です。「～する」と解釈しましょう。詳しくはGrammar Review 11（Chapter 11）を参照してください。

6) 関係詞節

関係詞節とは関係代名詞と関係副詞による節です。関係代名詞についてはGrammar Review 15（Chapter 15）を、関係副詞についてはGrammar Review 16（Chapter 16）を参照してください。

Exercises for the TOEIC® L&R Test

Part 5 Select the best answer to complete each sentence.

1. Look at that ______ window! Who did it?
(A) breaking
(B) broken
(C) break
(D) to break

2. The number of ______ mothers is increasing in our office.
(A) working
(B) work
(C) worked
(D) to work

3. This is the restaurant ______ opened in this neighborhood recently.
(A) it
(B) which
(C) and
(D) where

4. I can't go out for dinner. I have a lot of work ______ today.
(A) finished
(B) finishing
(C) to finish
(D) finish

5. Chinatown ______ Yokohama attracts many people who love Chinese food.
(A) from
(B) on
(C) for
(D) in

Part 6 Select the best answer to complete the text.

Restaurant Reviews

Four Seasons Seafood Restaurant

This restaurant is a seafood chain that can be found all over the United States. Everything is delicious, but I decided to have a crab sandwich for my meal. It is the most popular dish in the restaurant. I had it together **–1–** clam chowder. **–2–**. It went well with the soup. The atmosphere of the restaurant and the staff were very nice. All of the restaurant's menu items **–3–** listed with their calories, so people **–4–** about calories can order without worry.

1. (A) with
(B) without
(C) of
(D) at

2. (A) The sandwich was a perfect combination of tomato and crab.
(B) The next place we visited was a restaurant in Hawaii.
(C) With our stomachs full, we walked towards downtown Manhattan.
(D) If you show that card at the register, you can get a free drink.

3. (A) be
(B) is
(C) was
(D) are

4. (A) concerns
(B) concerned
(C) is concerned
(D) are concerned

Part 7 Read the announcement and choose the best answer to each question.

A dining experience you can't forget!

We are pleased to announce the opening of Charlie's Dining Bar. We offer a wide variety of organic dishes cooked with locally grown ingredients. We are confident that you will enjoy your meal and drinks while relaxing in our natural-taste interior.

All our staff is looking forward to serving you! We have also enclosed a $10 service coupon to celebrate the opening.

For more information, visit our website shown below.

＊＊＊

Date of opening: May 1
Business hours: 11:00 A.M. – 9:00 P.M. (Closed on Wednesdays)
Phone: 8081-937-7575
Email: charliesdb@sbb.com
Web site: www.chaliesdining.com

＊＊＊

To reserve a seat, please call or go online.

1. What kind of business is being advertised?
   (A) A restaurant
   (B) A farm
   (C) An interior decorating shop
   (D) A movie theater

2. The word "confident" in paragraph 1, line 3 is closest in meaning to
   (A) sorry
   (B) proud
   (C) sure
   (D) happy

CHAPTER 3

文と文の接続

Employment

本章での学習

▶文法：「文と文の接続」の復習・確認
▶話題：Employment
▶演習：Part 5 → Part 1 → Part 2 → Part 3 → Part 4形式の問題演習

事前学習

① Vocabulary 3とGrammar 3の問題に解答し、「語彙・文法クイズ」に備える。
② Part 3の音声を聞き、ディクテーション（書き取り）をする。

語彙・文法クイズ

Vocabulary 1 ～ 3とGrammar 1 ～ 3から5問（日本語→英語）

Vocabulary 3

Audio① 20

1 ～ 10の語句を英語にしましょう。その後で音声を聞いて確認しましょう。

1. 旅行代理店　________ agency
2. 就職の面接試験　________ interview
3. 求人に申し込む　apply for the ________
4. 履歴書を書く　write a ________
5. セキュリティ上の理由で　for ________ reasons
6. コピー機を使う　use a ________
7. 新入社員　new ________
8. 監督者　________
9. ～に焦点を当てる　________ on ～
10. 人事部　Human Resources ________

Grammar 3

1 ～ 5の空所を埋めましょう。その後で、音声を聞いて確認しましょう。

1. 子どものときにはゲームクリエーターになりたいと思っていました。
   I wanted to be a game creator ________ I was a child.

2. 私は旅行が好きなので、旅行代理店で働きたい。
   I want to work for a travel agency ____________ I like traveling.

3. もし金曜日の都合がよければ、面接試験を行いたいと思います。
   We would like to have an interview ________ Friday is good for you.

4. 小さな会社ですが、私には魅力的です。
   ____________ it's a small company, it's attractive to me.

5. たとえ給料がよくなくても、私はそこで働きたいです。
   ______________ they don't pay well, I'd like to work for them.

Pair Practice

・Vocabulary 3を、瞬時に「日本語→英語」にできるように、ペア(AとB)を組んで練習しましょう(1分間)。1分後にAとBの役割を交換し、同様に練習しましょう(1分間)。

A: 教科書を見ながらBに日本語を与える

B: 教科書を閉じたままAが与える日本語を英語にする

A: Bが即答できなければ、すぐにその英語を教え、1分間の内にどの語句もスラスラ英語で言えるようにさせる

・Grammar 3の例文についても同様の練習をしましょう(1分間)。

Grammar Review 3

文と文の接続

1) 主役の文 + 接続詞 + 主役の文
I like jazz **and** Ayaka likes K-pop.

2) 主役の文 + [接続詞 + 脇役の文]
We'll go to the beach tomorrow **if** it is sunny.

英語の文と文は、上の(1)、(2)のいずれかの形で接続され、その関係は接続詞の意味が決定します。(1)は等位接続と呼ばれ、主な接続詞はand, or, butなどです。一方、(2)は従属接続と呼ばれます。この接続は、前後が入れ代わって、[接続詞 + 脇役の文], 主役の文 という形でもOK。従属接続詞にはif, when, though, as, while, onceなどをはじめ、数多くあります。以下、従属接続について、空所を埋めながら整理してみましょう。

1) 時	接続詞： when, while, as, before, after, until, as soon asなど Give me a call ＿＿＿＿＿ you arrive at the station. (電話をください／駅に着いたときに)
2) 原因、理由	接続詞： because, since, as, now thatなど I'm late ＿＿＿＿＿＿ the train was delayed. (遅刻しました／電車が遅延したので)
3) 条件	接続詞： if, unless, in case, once など We'll go to the beach tomorrow ＿＿＿ it is sunny. (私たちは明日、海に行きます／もし晴れれば) We'll go to the beach tomorrow ＿＿＿＿＿＿ it rains. (私たちは明日、海に行きます／雨が降らない限り)
4) 譲歩	接続詞： though, although, even if, even thoughなど ＿＿＿＿＿＿ it's raining, we'll go to the beach. (雨が降っているけれども、私たちは海に行きます) ＿＿＿＿＿＿ it rains, we'll go to the beach. (たとえ雨が降っても、私たちは海に行きます)
5) その他	目的： so thatなど Speak louder ＿＿＿＿＿＿＿ everybody can hear you. (もっと大きな声で話してください／みんなに聞こえるように) 結果：so (such) ~ that ... (とても～なので…だ) 様態：**As** you know, ... (ご存知のように、…) 範囲：**As far as** I know, ... (私の知る限り、…) **as long as** the weather permits (天気が許す限り) ≒ if ...

▶従属接続詞

前の表で意味と例文が示されていないものをここに追加します。例文を通して、「主役の文」と「脇役の文」の関係を確認しましょう。

1)「時」を表す従属接続詞

- while ...（…している間に）
  He came while you were out.（彼が来た／あなたが出かけている間に）
- as ...（…と同時に）
  Use a dictionary as you read.（辞書を使いなさい／読むと同時に）
- after ...（…した後で）
  I'll clean my room after I finish my homework.（部屋の掃除をします／宿題を終えた後で）
- before ...（…する前に）
  Clean your room before you do your homework.（部屋の掃除をしなさい／宿題をやる前に）
- as soon as ...（…するや否や）
  I'll go out as soon as I finish my homework.（出かけます／宿題を終えたらすぐに）
- until / till ...（…するまでずっと）
  Wait here until I come back.（ここで待っていて／私が戻ってくるまで）

2)「原因・理由」を表す従属接続詞

- since ...（…なので）
  Since it's Friday, let's not work overtime.（金曜日なので、残業はやめましょう）
- as ...（…なので）
  Tell them what to do as you are the leader.（彼らに指示して／あなたはリーダーなのだから）
  ＊sinceとasは、相手がすでに知っていると思われる原因・理由を述べるときに使う。
- now that ...（今や…だから）
  Now that you are twenty, you can drink.（二十歳になったのだから、お酒が飲めるね）

3)「条件」を表す従属接続詞

- in case ...（…の場合に、…の場合に備えて）
  The game will be canceled in case it rains.（試合は中止になります／雨が降った場合）
  Take an umbrella with you in case it rains.（傘を持っていきなさい／雨に備えて）
- once ...（いったん…したら）
  Once you learn it, you'll never forget it.（いったん覚えたら、忘れることはない）

4) 「譲歩」を表す従属接続詞

・although ...（…だけれども）：thoughと同じ

・even though ...（…だけれども）：thoughの強調形

5) その他

・so ~ that ...（とても～なので …）

She was so tired that she couldn't cook.（彼女はとても疲れていたので食事を作れなかった）

Exercises for the TOEIC® L&R Test

Part 5 Select the best answer to complete each sentence.

1. Make a copy of the application ______ you lose it.
(A) as
(B) in case
(C) though
(D) until

2. I was ______ nervous at the job interview that I couldn't answer well.
(A) so
(B) little
(C) much
(D) as

3. You will have a better chance of employment ______ you can speak Chinese.
(A) and
(B) if
(C) though
(D) as soon as

4. ______ you are a third-year student, you should begin job hunting.
(A) But
(B) Unless
(C) Now that
(D) In case

5. I will work for an IT company for some years ______ I start up my own business.
(A) since
(B) because
(C) when
(D) until

Part 1 Listen and select the one statement that best describes what you see in the picture. **Audio① 22-24**

1.

Ⓐ Ⓑ Ⓒ Ⓓ

2.

Ⓐ Ⓑ Ⓒ Ⓓ

Part 2 Listen and select the best response to each question or statement. **Audio① 25-29**

1. Ⓐ Ⓑ Ⓒ 2. Ⓐ Ⓑ Ⓒ 3. Ⓐ Ⓑ Ⓒ 4. Ⓐ Ⓑ Ⓒ

Part 3 Listen and select the best answer to each question. **Audio① 30-32**

1. Who is the man?
   (A) A repair man
   (B) A system engineer
   (C) A new employee
   (D) A security officer

2. Why can't the man use his private computer?
   (A) Because it is too heavy
   (B) Because it is not safe
   (C) Because it is too expensive
   (D) Because it is usually locked

3. Where can the man make copies?
   (A) Room 201
   (B) Room 301
   (C) Room 401
   (D) Room 501

Part 4 Listen and select the best answer to each question. Audio① 33-35

1. Who are the listeners?
   (A) Personnel staff
   (B) New staff
   (C) Trainers
   (D) Supervisors

2. How long will the basic training be?
   (A) Three days
   (B) Four days
   (C) Five days
   (D) Six days

3. Who will be talking next?
   (A) A personnel staff member
   (B) A sales staff member
   (C) A publicity staff member
   (D) A marketing staff member

CHAPTER 4

進行形と受動態

Communication

本章での学習

▶文法：「進行形」と「受動態」の復習・確認
▶話題：Communication
▶演習：Part 5 → Part 6 → Part 7形式の問題演習

事前学習

① Vocabulary 4とGrammar 4の問題に解答し、「語彙・文法クイズ」に備える。
② Part 7の英文(2つ目)をチャンク単位で全文和訳をする。

語彙・文法クイズ

Vocabulary 1 ～ 4とGrammar 1 ～ 4から5問(日本語→英語)

Vocabulary 4

Audio① 36

1 ～ 10の語句を英語にしましょう。その後で音声を聞いて確認しましょう。

1. オートバイを製造する　＿＿＿＿＿＿ motorcycles
2. 自分(あなた自身)を理解してもらう　＿＿＿＿ yourself understood
3. 目標を達成する　＿＿＿＿＿ a goal
4. ～をフル活用する　make full ＿＿＿＿ of ～
5. 非言語コミュニケーション手段　non-verbal ＿＿＿＿ of communication
6. ～に任命される　be ＿＿＿＿＿ for ～
7. 何とかして～を切り抜ける　manage to ＿＿＿＿ through ～
8. 私は行き詰っている。　I am ＿＿＿＿＿ .
9. あなたに直接(会って)尋ねる　ask you in ＿＿＿＿＿
10. 同僚　＿＿＿＿＿

Grammar 4

Audio① 37

1 ～ 5の空所を埋めましょう。その後で、音声を聞いて確認しましょう。

1. 今月は家からオンラインで仕事をしています。

   I am ____________ online from home this month.

2. 英語がグローバルビジネスのコミュニケーションに使われています。

   English is _________ for global business communication.

3. どちらさまでしょうか(電話)。

   Who is ____________ ?

4. 毎日50通以上のEメールが私に送られてきます。

   More than 50 e-mails are _________ to me every day.

5. スケジュールは来週発表されるでしょう。

   The schedule will _______ announced next week.

Pair Practice

・Vocabulary 4を、瞬時に「日本語→英語」にできるように、ペア(AとB)を組んで練習しましょう(1分間)。1分後にAとBの役割を交換し、同様に練習しましょう(1分間)。

A: 教科書を見ながらBに日本語を与える

B: 教科書を閉じたままAが与える日本語を英語にする

A: Bが即答できなければ、すぐにその英語を教え、1分間の内にどの語句もスラスラ英語で言えるようにさせる

・Grammar 4の例文についても同様の練習をしましょう(1分間)。

Grammar Review 4

進行形と受動態

進行形: 何は(主語) + ～している(be + ～ ing) + ………

受動態: 何は(主語) + ～される(be + 過去分詞) + ……… + (by ～)

英語の進行形は動詞(どうする)の部分を「be動詞＋現在分詞(~ing)」にすることで「～している」、「受動態(受け身)」は「be動詞＋過去分詞」にすることで「～される」と表現できます。空所を埋めながら整理しましょう。

■ 進行形

現在進行形	She ______________ on the phone now. (彼女は今、電話で話しています)
過去進行形	She ______________ on the phone when I came home. (彼女は電話で話していました／私が帰宅したとき)

■ 受動態

文　型	能動態(～する) → 受動態(～される)
1. SVOの場合	A dog bit me. → I ______________ by a dog. (私は噛まれた／犬に)
2. SVOOの場合	The teacher gave students some hints. → Students ______________ some hints by the teacher. (生徒たちは与えられた／いくつかヒントを／先生によって) → Some hints ______________ **to** students by the teacher. (いつかヒントが与えられた／生徒たちに／先生によって)
3. SVOCの場合	Her smile made me happy. → I ______________ happy by her smile. (私は幸せな気分になった／彼女のほほ笑みで)
4. SVO+動詞原形の場合	Some people saw him enter the room. → He ______________ **to** enter the room by some people. (彼は目撃された／その部屋に入っていくのを／何人かの人に)
5. 群動詞の場合	My friend will take care of our cat while we are away. → Our cat will ______________________ by my friend while we are away. (我が家のネコは世話をされる／友人に／私たちが留守の間)

6. 進行形の場合	Cabin attendants are taking orders now. → Orders ＿＿＿＿＿＿＿＿＿＿ now by cabin attendants. （オーダーが今、取られている／客室乗務員によって）
7. 完了形の場合	He has written more than 100 songs so far. → More than 100 songs ＿＿＿＿＿＿＿＿＿＿ by him so far. （100曲以上が書かれてきた／彼によって／今まで）
8. by ～が不在	(1) 行為者がわからない場合 My passport ＿＿＿＿＿＿＿ in the airport. （パスポートが盗まれた／空港で） (2) 行為者をあえて示す必要がない場合など English ＿＿＿＿＿＿ as an official language in Singapore. （英語が話されている／公用語として／シンガポールでは）

▶受動態：動詞の部分の変化

前の表は、受動態がどのような文型でどのように作られるか、それを整理するため機械的に能動態から受動態に書き変えたものです。表の1 ～ 7の例文の、動詞の部分がどのように変化したのかを順に解説します。

1. 能動態： A dog bit me.
   動詞　：bite（噛む）→ be bitten（噛まれる）→ was bitten（噛まれた）
   受動態：I was bitten by a dog.

2. 能動態： The teacher gave students some hints.
   動詞　：give（与える）→ be given（与えられる）→ were given（与えられた）
   受動態：目的語が２つあるので2つの受動態の文ができる
   1）Students were given some hints by the teacher.
   2）Some hints were given to students by the teacher.
   ＊studentsがto studentsとなることに注意

3. 能動態： Her smile made me happy.
   動詞　：make（させる）→ be made（させられる）→ was made（させられた）
   受動態：I was made happy by her smile.

4. 能動態：Some people saw him enter the room.
動詞　：see（見る）→ be seen（みられる）→ was seen（見られた）
受動態：He was seen to enter the room by some people.
＊この文型では原形不定詞(enter)がto不定詞(to enter)になる

5. 能動態：My friend will take care of our cat while we are away.
動詞　：take care of（世話をする）→ be taken care of（世話をされる）
→ will be taken care of（世話をされるでしょう）
受動態：Our cat will be taken care of by my friend while we are away.

6. 能動態：Cabin attendants are taking orders now.
動詞　：take（取る）→ be taken（取られる）→ are being taken（取られている）
受動態：Orders are being taken now by cabin attendants.

7. 能動態：He has written more than 100 songs so far.
動詞　：write（書く）→ be written（書かれる）→ have been written（書かれてきた）
受動態：More than 100 songs have been written by him so far.

8. 能動態：Someone stole my passport in the airport.
動詞　：steal（盗む）→ be stolen（盗まれる）→ was stolen（盗まれた）
受動態：My passport was stolen (by someone) in the airport.
＊by someoneは省略される

能動態：People speak English as an official language in Singapore.
動詞　：speak（話す）→ be spoken（話される）→ is spoken（話される）
受動態：English is spoken (by people) as an official language in Singapore.
＊by peopleは省略される

Exercises for the TOEIC® L&R Test

Part 5 Select the best answer to complete each sentence.

1. Social networking services such as Facebook and Instagram _______ by many young people.
(A) uses
(B) are used
(C) is used
(D) are using

2. The number of remote workers _______ in many countries around the world.
(A) is increasing
(B) to increase
(C) increase
(D) are increasing

3. I'm sorry, but the price has not _______ yet.
(A) be decided
(B) been decided
(C) is deciding
(D) was deciding

4. Last year, more than 50 percent of the world's motorcycles _______ in China.
(A) are manufactured
(B) manufactured
(C) were manufactured
(D) were manufacturing

5. Global businesspeople _______ on the Internet 24 hours a day.
(A) needs connection
(B) need to connecting
(C) needs to connect
(D) need to be connected

Part 6 Select the best answer to complete the text.

It is **−1−** that you need a good skill in English to communicate with people from other countries. It is true but English is only a tool for communication. The goal is not to speak English, but to communicate with others to make yourself understood. In **−2−** to achieve this goal, it is important to communicate by making full use of both verbal and non-verbal means of communication.

−3−. One of them is an eye contact. Some people are not confident in their English. So they don't look the other person in the eye. **−4−** thing is the volume of the voice. Some people speak in a very quiet voice. Maybe you have experienced something like this yourself.

1. (A) say
   (B) saying
   (C) said
   (D) to say

2. (A) spite
   (B) case
   (C) order
   (D) front

3. (A) There are many ways to do this.
   (B) It's hard to communicate with them.
   (C) However, it is possible to communicate in Japanese.
   (D) It is very difficult for Japanese people to learn a foreign language!

4. (A) One
   (B) Other
   (C) Some
   (D) Another

Part 7 Read the e-mails and choose the best answer to each question.

To: Mike Johnson
From: Sue Leach
Date: June 17
Subject: How are you doing?

Hi Mike,

How are you getting ready for your project? I understand that this is your first project as a leader and I heard from John that you were having some problems.

When I was selected as a project manager for the first time, I had a hard time, too. I didn't have any knowledge about it. Luckily, there were many people around me who helped me, so I managed to get through it.

This project is not a big one, but I think it will be a good experience for you. If there is anything I can do to help you, you are always welcome to contact me.

Sue

To: Sue Leach
From: Mike Johnson
Date: June 18
Subject: Re: How are you doing?

Hi Sue,

Thank you very much for your concern about my project.

Actually, I am stuck due to lack of experience, just like you were. I have a lot of questions, so I think it would be quicker to ask you in person than in writing.

I will be visiting the head office next Monday to attend a meeting. If I can talk to you then, it will help me a lot. I'm free after 3:00.

Thank you again.

Mike

1. What is the purpose of the first e-mail?
   (A) To offer help
   (B) To arrange a meeting
   (C) To prepare for a party
   (D) To start a project

2. Who probably is Sue?
   (A) Mike's colleague
   (B) Mike's teacher
   (C) Mike's girlfriend
   (D) Mike's client

3. In the second e-mail, the expression "due to" in paragraph 2, line 1, is closest in meaning to
   (A) because of
   (B) thanks to
   (C) instead of
   (D) according to

4. Where does Sue work?
   (A) At the same office as Mike
   (B) At a branch office
   (C) At the headquarters
   (D) At home

5. When will Mike probably be meeting Sue?
   (A) In the morning
   (B) At lunch time
   (C) In the afternoon
   (D) In the evening

CHAPTER 5

知覚動詞と使役動詞

Transportation

本章での学習

▶文法：知覚動詞と使役動詞の復習・確認
▶話題：Transportation
▶演習：Part 5 → Part 1 → Part 2 → Part 3 → Part 4形式の問題演習

事前学習

① Vocabulary 5とGrammar 5の問題に解答し、「語彙・文法クイズ」に備える。
② Part 3の音声を聞き、ディクテーション（書き取り）をする。

語彙・文法クイズ

Vocabulary 1 ～ 5とGrammar 1 ～ 5から5問（日本語→英語）

Vocabulary 5

Audio① 38

1～10の語句を英語にしましょう。その後で音声を聞いて確認しましょう。

1. 休暇を3日とる　＿＿＿＿ three days off
2. トラックに荷物を積む　＿＿＿＿ the truck
3. 空港に（車で）あなたを迎えに行く　＿＿＿＿ you up at the airport
4. それを修理してもらう　have it ＿＿＿＿
5. 展示会場　＿＿＿＿ site
6. 電気料金　electricity ＿＿＿＿
7. もう少し待ってもらえますか。　Can you ＿＿＿＿ on a little longer?
8. 救急車　＿＿＿＿
9. 高速道路の交通渋滞　＿＿＿＿ traffic on the expressway
10. ～のかなり前に　well in ＿＿＿＿ of ～

Grammar 5

Audio① 39

1 ～ 5の空所を埋めましょう。その後で、音声を聞いて確認しましょう。

1. あなたのお父さんが急いで駅に走っていくのを見ました。
   I saw your father ____________ to the station.

2. 次の列車が何時に出るか教えて頂けますか。
   _________ me know when the next train will leave.

3. 彼は秘書にニューヨークへの飛行機を予約してもらった。
   He _________ his secretary book a flight to New York.

4. あなたの名前が呼ばれるのを聞きましたか。
   Did you hear your name ____________ ?

5. どうもパスポートを盗まれたようだ。
   I'm afraid I _________ my passport stolen.

Pair Practice

・Vocabulary 5を、瞬時に「日本語→英語」にできるように、ペア（AとB）を組んで練習しましょう（1分間）。1分後にAとBの役割を交換し、同様に練習しましょう（1分間）。

A: 教科書を見ながらBに日本語を与える

B: 教科書を閉じたままAが与える日本語を英語にする

A: Bが即答できなければ、すぐにその英語を教え、1分間の内にどの語句もスラスラ英語で言えるようにさせる

・Grammar 5の例文についても同様の練習をしましょう（1分間）。

Grammar Review 5

知覚動詞と使役動詞

英語の文型で注意を要するものに、「見る」「聞く」「感じる」などの知覚動詞(see, hear, feelなど)と、「〜させる」「〜させてやる」「〜してもらう」を意味する使役動詞(make, let, have, getなど)によって作られる文型があります。例文の空所を埋めながら、確認と整理をしましょう。

知覚動詞(see, hear, feel など)

主語 ＋ 知覚動詞 ＋ 目的語 ＋ { 1) 原形不定詞(〜する) / 2) 現在分詞(〜している) / 3) 過去分詞(〜される) }

1)	I 私は	**heard** 聞いた	someone 誰かが	________ 呼ぶのを	my name. 私の名前を
2)	I 私は	**heard** 聞いた	someone 誰かが	________ 呼んでいるのを	my name. 私の名前を
3)	I 私は	**heard** 聞いた	my name 私の名前が	________ . 呼ばれるのを	

使役動詞(make, let, have + get)

主語(S) ＋ make/have/let ＋ 目的語(O) ＋ 原形不定詞	
1. make 強制	SはOに〜させる I **made** him ________ there.(私は彼をそこに行かせた)
2. let 許可	SはOに〜させてやる I **let** him ________ there.(私は彼をそこに行かせてやった)
3. have 中間	SはOに〜してもらう(させる) I **had** him ________ there.(私は彼にそこに行ってもらった)
4. get 努力・説得	【S ＋ get ＋ O ＋ **to**不定詞】 SはOに〜させる I **got** him ________ there.(私は彼をそこに行かせた)

主語(S) ＋ have/get ＋ 目的語(O) ＋ 過去分詞	
1. have	Sはhaveする → [Oが〜される] を I **had** my hair ________ .(私は髪を染めてもらった) I **had** my bike ________ .(私は自転車を盗まれた)
2. get	Sはget する → [Oが〜される] を I'll **get** this ________ by Friday.(金曜までにこれを終わらせておきます)

▶知覚動詞

知覚動詞にはsee, hear, feel の他に、watch, listen to, notice などがあります。いずれも前の表に挙げた形で使うことができます。

▶使役動詞

使役動詞 make, let, have, get は「(人) に～させる」という大枠の意味では共通していますが、実はそれぞれ下に示すような異なった意味を含みます。

1. make:「(強制的に) ～させる」

I made him go there. では、「彼」がそこに行きたくなかったかもしれないが、彼の意思に関わらず「行かせた」という意味。

2. let:「(許可を与えて) ～させてやる」

I let him go there. では、「彼」がそこに行くことを望んでいて、「私」はそれを許可した、という意味。

3. have:「(中間的に) ～させる／してもらう」

・日本語にこの「中間的」なhaveに相当する表現がないため、「～してもらう」と訳したり「～させる」と訳したりします。どちらにするかは文脈で決めます。
・S＋have＋O＋過去分詞のパターンでも同様の問題が生じます。ここでも文脈による判断が求められます。I had my hair dyed.では、本人の利益になるので「～してもらう」。I had my bike stolen.では、本人の不利益になるので、今度は「～される」と解釈します。

4. get:「(努力・説得して) ～させる」

I got him to go there.では、「彼」がそこに行くことに気が進まなかったのかもしれません。そこを「私」が説得して「行かせた」という意味。

Exercises for the TOEIC® L&R Test

Part 5 Select the best answer to complete each sentence.

1. I saw many people ______ in line at the bus stop this morning.
(A) to wait
(B) waiting
(C) take
(D) calling

2. I'll get my client ______ the schedule.
(A) to change
(B) changing
(C) changed
(D) change

3. His boss ________ Tom take three days off after his long business trip to Europe.
(A) allowed
(B) let
(C) gave
(D) got

4. Cruising in the bad weather ______ me feel sick.
(A) had
(B) let
(C) made
(D) got

5. I called the airline company and had my flight reservation ______ .
(A) cancelation
(B) canceling
(C) to cancel
(D) canceled

Part 1 Listen and select the one statement that best describes what you see in the picture. Audio① 40-42

1.

Ⓐ Ⓑ Ⓒ Ⓓ

2.

Ⓐ Ⓑ Ⓒ Ⓓ

Part 2 Listen and select the best response to each question or statement. Audio① 43-47

1. Ⓐ Ⓑ Ⓒ   2. Ⓐ Ⓑ Ⓒ   3. Ⓐ Ⓑ Ⓒ   4. Ⓐ Ⓑ Ⓒ

Part 3 Listen and select the best answer to each question. Audio① 48-50

1. Where are they talking?
   (A) On the train
   (B) On the bus
   (C) At a bus stop
   (D) At a hospital

2. How long does the driver say it will take to the next bus stop?
   (A) About five minutes
   (B) About ten minutes
   (C) About fifteen minutes
   (D) About twenty minutes

3. Where does the woman probably work?
   (A) At a university
   (B) At a clinic
   (C) At a nursing school
   (D) At a bus company

Part 4 Listen and select the best answer to each question. Audio① 51-53

1. What kind of report is this?
(A) Weather
(B) Traffic
(C) Entertainment
(D) Flight

2. Why is West Street closed?
(A) Due to a traffic accident
(B) Due to a bad weather
(C) Due to a road construction
(D) Due to a special event

3. When will the next report be made?
(A) 7:00 A.M.
(B) 9:00 A.M.
(C) 1:00 P.M.
(D) 7:00 P.M.

CHAPTER 6

助動詞

Entertainment

本章での学習

▶文法：助動詞の復習・確認
▶話題：Entertainment
▶演習：Part 5 → Part 6 → Part 7形式の問題演習

事前学習

① Vocabulary 6とGrammar 6の問題に解答し、「語彙・文法クイズ」に備える。
② Part 7の英文をチャンク単位で全文和訳をする。

語彙・文法クイズ

Vocabulary 1 ～ 6とGrammar 1 ～ 6から5問（日本語→英語）

Vocabulary 6

Audio① 54

1～10の語句を英語にしましょう。その後で音声を聞いて確認しましょう。

1. 絶対に ________________
2. 顧客をもてなす ________________ clients
3. 宗教上の信仰のために ____________ to religious beliefs
4. あなたの心に浮かぶ ____________ to your mind
5. テーマパーク ____________ park
6. ～と言えば ______________ about ～
7. 聴衆 ________________
8. 違法な ______________
9. 10週連続で ten weeks in a ____________
10. 怖すぎて～できない too ______________ to ～

Grammar 6

Audio① 55

1～5の空所を埋めましょう。その後で、音声を聞いて確認しましょう。

1. 私はニンジンとピーマンが食べられません。

   I ________ eat carrots and green peppers.

2. 入ってもよろしいですか。

   ________ I come in?

3. すぐに行かないと電車に遅れるよ。

   You ________ go now, or you'll miss the train.

4. 手伝ってくれない？

   ________ you help me?

5. あなたは毎日運動をした方がいい。

   You ___________ exercise every day.

Pair Practice

・Vocabulary 6を、瞬時に「日本語→英語」にできるように、ペア（AとB）を組んで練習しましょう（1分間）。1分後にAとBの役割を交換し、同様に練習しましょう（1分間）。

A: 教科書を見ながらBに日本語を与える

B: 教科書を閉じたままAが与える日本語を英語にする

A: Bが即答できなければ、すぐにその英語を教え、1分間の内にどの語句もスラスラ英語で言えるようにさせる

・Grammar 6の例文についても同様の練習をしましょう（1分間）。

Grammar Review 6

助動詞

何が（主語）＋ 助動詞 どうする（動詞）＋ ……………… ＋α（副詞）

助動詞は、動詞にさまざまな意味合いを加える「調味料」のようなものです。文中では「どうする（動詞）」の直前に位置し、「どうする（動詞）」とセットになり述部を構成します。ここでは、助動詞の中でも頻繁に使用される代表的な５つの助動詞、can, may, must, will, shall について、空所を埋めながら整理・確認していきましょう。

1. can	可能（性）：「～することが可能」、「～する可能性がある」
過去形：could 代用：be able to	I ________ understand English, but I can't speak it well. （英語は理解できますが、上手に話すことはできません） **Can** I leave now? （もう帰ってもいいですか） Smoking **can** cause cancer. （喫煙は癌を引き起こす可能性があります） __________ you help me? 仮定法過去 （手伝っていただけますか）
2. may	**推量：「～かもしれない」、許可：「～してよい」**
過去形：might	She **may** come. （彼女は来るかもしれません） ________ I have your name, please? （お名前を伺ってもよろしいですか） She __________ come. 仮定法過去 （彼女はひょっとしたら来るかもしれません）
3. must	**不可避：「～しなければならない」、推定：「～に違いない」**
過去形：had to 代用：have to	It's 10:00. I **must** leave now. （10時だ。もう帰らないと） You ________ be kidding! （冗談でしょう！） She ___________ give up her dream of studying abroad. （彼女は留学の夢をあきらめなければならなかった）

4. will	意思：「〜する（つもり）」、推測：「〜するでしょう」
過去形：would	I **will** never forget you. （あなたのことは決して忘れません） I'm sure she **will** like it. （きっと彼女はそれを気に入るでしょうよ） ___________ you help me? 仮定法過去 （手伝ってもらえますか）
5. shall	**提案（疑問文で）：「〜しましょうか」、助言：「〜すべき」、推量：「〜するはず」**
過去形：should	**Shall** I open the window? （（私、）窓を開けましょうか） ___________ we begin first? （（私たち、）先に始めましょうか） You ___________ apologize to her. 仮定法過去 （あなたは彼女に謝るべきだ） It ___________ be on your desk. （それはあなたの机の上にあるはずです）

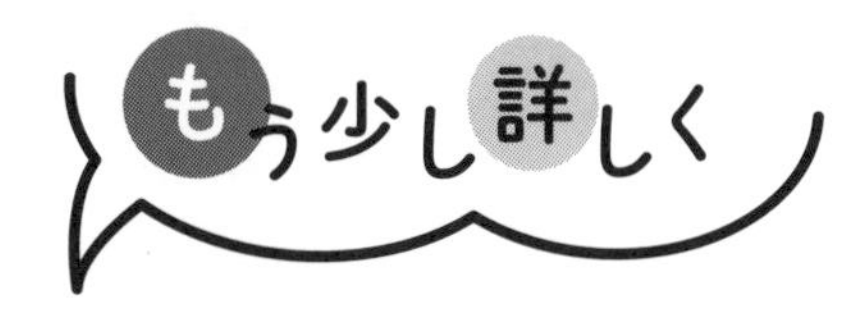

▶助動詞

助動詞は「調味料」なので、それぞれの「味」と使い方を理解すれば、自分の話す英語、書く英語を味わい深いものにすることができます。また、そのように話され書かれた英文を正しく味わうことができます。

▶助動詞の代用

表のcanとmust の欄に「代用」として書かれているbe able toとhave toについて説明を加えます。

1. canの代用： be able to

【未来などの表現で】 助動詞を２つ同時に使うことはできないので、例えば、未来の「可能」を表すときには will can ではなく、will be able toと表現します。

・She will be able to leave the hospital next week.（彼女は来週には退院できるでしょう）

2. mustの代用： have to

【未来などの表現で】 助動詞を２つ同時に使うことはできないので、例えば、未来の「不可避」を表す時には will must ではなく、will have toと表現します。

・I will have to write a paper tonight.（私は今晩レポートを書かなければならない）

【過去の表現で】mustには過去形がないので、過去の「不可避」を表す時にはhave toを過去形had toにして使います。

・He had to give up his dream.（彼は夢をあきらめなければならなかった）

▶助動詞の過去形

1. 過去を表す could, would

・I could not swim at all last year.（私は、去年は全く泳げませんでした）

・I thought he would come but he didn't.（彼は来るだろうと思ったのですが、来ませんでした）

2. 仮定法過去で使われるcould, might, would, should

文を読んでいて、現在の話なのになぜ突然couldやmight, would, shouldのような過去形が出てくるのだろうと思ったことはありませんか。それらは「仮定法過去」(Grammar Review 12参照）というルールから出てきた表現です。If S+V (過去形) ..., (もし…だったら) が省略されていると考え、「もし…だったら」の含みを加えて解釈します。

・Could you help me?

「(もし…だったら) あなたは私を手伝うことは可能ですか？」
例えば「もし時間があったら、あなたは私を手伝うことは可能ですか？」のように、「もし…だったら」という含みをcanに加えたものがcouldです。

・She might come.

「(もし…だったら) 彼女は来るかもしれない。」
「もし…だったら」という含みをmayに加えたものがmightです。

・Would you help me?

「(もし…だったら) あなたは私を手伝ってくれますか？」
「もし…だったら」という含みをwillに加えたものがwouldです。

・You should apologize to her.

「(もし…だったら) あなたは彼女に謝るべきです。」
「もし…だったら」という含みをshallに加えたものがshouldです。

Exercises for the TOEIC® L&R Test

Part 5 Select the best answer to complete each sentence.

1. If you go to New York, you definitely _______ see musicals on Broadway.
(A) has to
(B) may
(C) should
(D) might

2. _______ you know any good restaurants to entertain my clients from Vietnam?
(A) Can
(B) Will
(C) Must
(D) Do

3. _______ you help me read the menu? It's all written in French and I can't understand it at all.
(A) May
(B) Could
(C) Shall
(D) Must

4. You should be careful when you choose a restaurant. Some people _______ eat meat or drink alcohol due to their religious beliefs.
(A) cannot
(B) don't have to
(C) are able to
(D) should

5. Though we didn't reserve tickets for the football game, luckily we _______ get seats.
(A) might
(B) should
(C) would
(D) were able to

Part 6 Select the best answer to complete the text.

When you hear the word "entertainment," what **–1–** to your mind? Is it listening to music at a concert, watching TV, going to the movies, or playing video games? **–2–**. There are also many other types of entertainment such as watching plays, reading books, or going to theme parks. In some countries, gambling may also be regarded as a form of entertainment. What is your favorite kind of entertainment? Talking **–3–** entertainment, did you know that Michael Jackson **–4–** as "the world's most successful entertainer" in the Guinness World Records?

1. (A) comes
(B) goes
(C) takes
(D) puts

2. (A) Most people don't have enough time for entertainment.
(B) An important part of entertainment is the audience.
(C) Or is it watching sports like baseball or soccer?
(D) Some kinds of entertainment are now illegal in most countries.

3. (A) with
(B) about
(C) for
(D) among

4. (A) be listed
(B) is listed
(C) be listing
(D) is listing

Part 7 Read the text-message chain and choose the best answer to each question.

13:00 Daniel
Do you have any plans for this weekend?

13:02 Mia
No. Why?

13:02 Daniel
I'm thinking of going to see a movie. Would you like to come?

13:04 Mia
What kind?

13:05 Daniel
It's horror. It's been No. 1 in the movie rankings for ten weeks in a row. It must be really good.

13:07 Mia
Sorry, but I don't like horror movies.

13:08 Daniel
Oh, please! I'm too scared to go by myself!

13:08 Mia
You can't be serious.

1. What are they talking about?
(A) Watching a movie
(B) Eating out
(C) Going jogging
(D) Going to a sporting event

2. Why does Daniel want Mia to come with him?
(A) Because he likes her.
(B) Because he is afraid to go alone.
(C) Because he is lonely.
(D) Because she is a horror movie fan.

3. At 13:08, what does Mia mean when she writes, "You can't be serious"?
(A) You are not kind.
(B) You must be joking.
(C) You can trust me.
(D) You are so nice.

CHAPTER 7

その他の助動詞と「助動詞＋完了形」

Negotiating

本章での学習

▶文法：その他の助動詞と「助動詞＋完了形」の復習・確認
▶話題：Negotiating
▶演習：Part 5 → Part 1 → Part 2 → Part 3 → Part 4形式の問題演習

事前学習

① Vocabulary 7とGrammar 7の問題に解答し、「語彙・文法クイズ」に備える。
② Part 3の音声を聞き、ディクテーション（書き取り）をする。

語彙・文法クイズ

Vocabulary 1 ～ 7とGrammar 1 ～ 7から5問（日本語→英語）

Vocabulary 7

Audio① 56

1 ～ 10の語句を英語にしましょう。その後で音声を聞いて確認しましょう。

1. 契約条件を決める　＿＿＿＿＿＿ the terms of the contract
2. 供給業者からの見積もり　＿＿＿＿＿＿ from a supplier
3. 価格を下げる　＿＿＿＿＿＿ the price
4. テレビ会議　＿＿＿＿＿＿＿＿
5. 交渉を主導する　lead the ＿＿＿＿＿＿＿＿
6. 人事部、総務部　＿＿＿＿＿＿ section, ＿＿＿＿＿＿ affairs section
7. 営業部、企画部　＿＿＿＿＿ section, ＿＿＿＿＿＿ section
8. 議題　＿＿＿＿＿＿
9. スケジュールに目を通す　look ＿＿＿＿＿ a schedule
10. オフィス用品　office ＿＿＿＿＿＿＿

Grammar 7

1 ～ 5の空所を埋めましょう。その後で、音声を聞いて確認しましょう。

1. 私はかつてコンビニでバイトをしていました。

   I ________ to work part time at a convenience store.

2. それは提出する必要がありません。

   You don't ________ to submit it.

3. 彼はそれを勘違いしたに違いない。

   He ________ have misunderstood it.

4. あなたは当然謝るべきです。

   You __________ to apologize.

5. 私は財布を落としたかもしれない。

   I ________ have lost my wallet.

Pair Practice

・Vocabulary 7を、瞬時に「日本語→英語」にできるように、ペア(AとB)を組んで練習しましょう(1分間)。1分後にAとBの役割を交換し、同様に練習しましょう(1分間)。

A: 教科書を見ながらBに日本語を与える

B: 教科書を閉じたままAが与える日本語を英語にする

A: Bが即答できなければ、すぐにその英語を教え、1分間の内にどの語句もスラスラ英語で言えるようにさせる

・Grammar 7の例文についても同様の練習をしましょう(1分間)。

Grammar Review 7

その他の助動詞と「助動詞＋完了形」

1) need ~（〜する必要がある）　2) ought to ~（〜すべきだ、〜するはずだ）
3) used to ~（かつては〜していた）　4) 助動詞 ＋ have ~（過去分詞）

例文を見ながら、Grammar Review 6に挙げた以外の「その他の助動詞」と「助動詞＋完了形」について空所を埋めながら整理しましょう。

1) need ~	「〜する必要がある」：助動詞としては否定文と疑問文でときどき使われる（主にイギリス英語の用法）。
	You **need** not go. （あなたは行く必要はありません） 一般動詞のneedで表現すれば次のようになる。 You don't ____________ go. = You don't have to go.
2) ought to ~	「〜すべきだ、〜するはずだ」（shouldよりやや意味が強い）
	You **ought to** __________ her. （あなたは彼女に感謝すべきだ）
3) used to ~	「かつては〜していた」（「現在はそうでない」という含みがある）
	I **used to** hate exercise, but now I love it. （私は、以前は運動が大嫌いでしたが、今は大好きです）
4) 助動詞＋完了形	a) cannot have ~（過去分詞）：「〜したはずがない（可能性がない）」
	He **cannot have** _________ that. （彼がそんなことをしたはずがない）
	b) may have ~（過去分詞）：「〜したかもしれない」
	I may **have** _________ so. （私がそう言ったかもしれない）
	c) must have ~（過去分詞）：「〜したに違いない（したはずだ）」
	He **must have** done that. （彼がそれをしたに違いない）

▶助動詞 need

前ページの表の解説にあるように、助動詞としてのneedは主にイギリス英語の用法で、否定文と疑問文で使われることがあります。しかし、イギリスにおいても need は一般動詞として使うことの方が多く、need to ~（不定詞）のように使います。

・You need to go.（一般動詞のneedの肯定文）
・You don't need to go.（一般動詞のneedの否定文）
・Do you need to go?（一般動詞のneedの疑問文）

また、助動詞のneedには過去形がありません。したがって、過去の表現をする場合にも、一般動詞のneedを過去形neededにして needed to ~のように使います。

・I needed to go.（私は行く必要があった）

▶「義務・助言」を表すいろいろな表現

Grammar Review 6でのmust, have to, shouldやこのGrammar Review 7での need to, ought toはいずれも広義での「義務・助言」を表します。強制力の強さは概ね①から⑤の順になります。

【強い】 ① must → ② need to → ③ have to → ④ ought to → ⑤ should 【弱い】

① **must ~（～しなければならない）：You must explain it.**
mustは「不可避」なので「何が何でも～しなければならない」

② **need to ~（～する必要がある）：You need to explain it.**
needは「必要」なので「必ず～しなければならない」

③ **have to ~（～しなければならない）：You have to explain it.**
haveは「持っている」なので「～することを抱え持っている」

④ **ought to ~（～すべきだ）：You ought to explain it.**
oughtは「義務」なので「～する義務がある」

⑤ **should ~（～した方がよい）：You should explain it.**
shouldは「当然」で「（当然～することになるので）～した方がよい」

Exercises for the TOEIC® L&R Test

Part 5 Select the best answer to complete each sentence.

1. I think we _______ meet once again and decide the terms of the contract.
(A) used to
(B) may have
(C) have to
(D) are

2. First, we _______ look at the quotes from the three suppliers and compare.
(A) are going
(B) has to
(C) like
(D) should

3. Mr. Smith _______ forgotten the appointment because I sent him a reminder yesterday.
(A) should
(B) cannot have
(C) ought to
(D) had to

4. We don't _______ lower the price any more. They looked pretty satisfied with the price itself.
(A) need to
(B) be able to
(C) used to
(D) must

5. He _______ said it as a joke, so it's nothing for you to get angry about.
(A) must have
(B) ought to
(C) would
(D) didn't

Part 1 Listen and select the one statement that best describes what you see in the picture. **Audio① 58-60**

1.

Ⓐ Ⓑ Ⓒ Ⓓ

2.

Ⓐ Ⓑ Ⓒ Ⓓ

Part 2 Listen and select the best response to each question or statement. **Audio① 61-65**

1. Ⓐ Ⓑ Ⓒ　2. Ⓐ Ⓑ Ⓒ　3. Ⓐ Ⓑ Ⓒ　4. Ⓐ Ⓑ Ⓒ

Part 3 Listen and select the best answer to each question. **Audio① 66-68**

Time	Agenda	Presenter
1:00-2:00	Future policies of the Personnel Section	Lu Baker
2:00-3:00	Sales target for this year	Margaret Anderson
3:00-4:00	General Affairs Section Policy for this year	George Jackson
4:00-5:00	New System for the Planning Section	Beth White

1. Why is the man calling?
   (A) To make a request
   (B) To reserve a room
   (C) To make an apology
   (D) To place an order

2. Look at the graphic. Which section does Ms. Anderson most likely work in?
   (A) General Affairs　(B) Sales　(C) Personnel　(D) Planning

3. What does Mr. Jackson need to do at 3:00?
   (A) Visit a client
   (B) Participate in another meeting
   (C) Go on a business trip
   (D) Leave the office

Part 4 Listen and select the best answer to each question. **Audio① 69-71**

Company	Price/set
AGA Group	$350
Beta Co., Ltd.	$370
Continental Services	$375
D's Co., Inc.	$398

1. What is the speaker asking for?
(A) A discount
(B) An opinion
(C) A price list
(D) A demonstration

2. Look at the graphic. Which company does Mr. Peterson work for?
(A) AGA Group
(B) Beta Co., Ltd.
(C) Continental Services
(D) D's Co., Inc.

3. What is most important for the speaker's boss?
(A) Price
(B) Quality
(C) After-sales service
(D) Delivery date

CHAPTER 8

時制（現在・過去・未来）

Giving a Presentation

本章での学習

▶文法：時制（現在・過去・未来）の復習・確認
▶話題：Giving a Presentation
▶演習：Part 5 → Part 6 → Part 7形式の問題演習

事前学習

① Vocabulary 8とGrammar 8の問題に解答し、「語彙・文法クイズ」に備える。
② Part 7の英文（1つ目）をチャンク単位で全文和訳する。

語彙・文法クイズ

Vocabulary 1 〜 8とGrammar 1 〜 8から5問（日本語→英語）

Vocabulary 8

Audio① 72

1 〜 10の語句を英語にしましょう。その後で音声を聞いて確認しましょう。

1. リストによると、… ________ to the list, ...
2. プレゼンの配布資料 ________ for a presentation
3. 顕著な増加 significant ________
4. 並外れた努力 remarkable ________
5. 業績に基づいて ________ on achievements
6. あなたはいつ都合がつきますか。 When will you be ________ ?
7. 原稿を作成する make a ________
8. プロジェクトに取り組む ________ on a project
9. 3機能を備えた加湿器 humidifier with three ________
10. 営業担当者 ________ representative

Grammar 8

Audio① 73

1 ～ 5の空所を埋めましょう。その後で、音声を聞いて確認しましょう。

1. 今週末、あなたは何をする予定ですか。
   What are you ___________ to do this weekend?

2. おそらく彼女は来ないでしょう。
   Perhaps, she _________ not come.

3. 今度の金曜日は図書館で勉強することになっています。
   I will _________ studying at the library this Friday.

4. 来週、5つ試験を受けることになっています。
   I’m ____________ five exams next week.

5. もし明日天気がよければ、私たちは海に行きます。
   If it _________ sunny tomorrow, we will go to the beach.

Pair Practice

・Vocabulary 8を、瞬時に「日本語→英語」にできるように、ペア（AとB）を組んで練習しましょう（1分間）。1分後にAとBの役割を交換し、同様に練習しましょう（1分間）。

A: 教科書を見ながらBに日本語を与える

B: 教科書を閉じたままAが与える日本語を英語にする

A: Bが即答できなければ、すぐにその英語を教え、1分間の内にどの語句もスラスラ英語で言えるようにさせる

・Grammar 8の例文についても同様の練習をしましょう（1分間）。

Grammar Review 8

時制（現在・過去・未来）

何が（主語）＋ { どうする　（動詞の現在形）
どうした　（動詞の過去形）
どうするだろう（will＋動詞の原形） } ＋ ……… ＋α（副詞）

英語の現在と過去は、「どうする（動詞）」を現在形ないし過去形にすることで表現できます。また、未来についても、動詞（原形）の前にwillを置くことで表現できます。ただ、未来については他にもいくつか表現方法がありますので、空所を埋めながら整理と確認をしましょう。

1. 現在	I work for a trading company in Tokyo. （私は東京の商社で働いています）
2. 過去	I ______________ overtime yesterday. （私は昨日残業しました）
	1）確定的未来：～（～する）
	I work tomorrow.（私は明日働きます）
	2）予測（単純・意志未来）：will ～（～するでしょう／～するつもり）
	I __________ work tomorrow.（私は明日働くでしょう／働くつもりです）
	3）予定（根拠）のある未来：be going to ～（～する予定／～することになる）
3. 未来	I am going to __________ tomorrow.（私は明日働く予定です） It's already 5:00. I am going to work overtime today. （もう5時だ。今日は残業することになる）
	4）近接未来：be ~ing（～することになっている）
	I __________ working tomorrow.（私は明日働くことになっています）
	5）予測＋近接未来：will be ~ing（～することになるでしょう）
	I will be working tomorrow.（私は明日働くことになるでしょう）
	6）予定＋近接未来：be going to be ~ing（予定では～することになっています）
	I am going to be working tomorrow.（私は予定では明日働くことになっています）
注意 未来でも 現在形	We will begin when she ____________ .（私たちは始めます／彼女が来たら） If you __________ busy tomorrow, I will help you. （明日忙しければ、私が手伝います）

▶未来の表現

未来のことは will や be going to で表現することが多いです。しかし、前の表で示したように他にもいろいろあります。まずは willとbe going toの使い分けができるようにしましょう。ついでに、他の表現についても知っておきましょう。

1) 確定的未来：現在形＋未来の副詞（〜します）

I work tomorrow.

動詞workの前に助動詞（調味料）のようなものは付いていません。したがって、淡々と「明日働きます」という意味です。

・確定的未来：変更の可能性がなく確定しているとき

2) 予測（単純・意志未来）：will ~（〜するでしょう／〜するつもりです）

① He will work tomorrow.

② I will work tomorrow.

動詞work前に助動詞 willが付いています。willは「〜するでしょう」（単純未来）と「〜するつもりです」（意志未来）を意味します。

・単純未来：一般に未来を表すとき

・意志未来：基本的に主語が「一人称」（I, weなど）のとき

3) 予定（根拠）のある未来：be going to ~（〜する予定／〜することになる）

① I am going to work tomorrow.

② It's already 5:00. I am going to work overtime today.

動詞 workの前にbe going toが付いています。もし、I am going to Shinjuku. だったら「新宿に向かってgoしている」（進行形）。このShinjukuがwork（働く）に入れ替わったと考えましょう。「仕事をする方向に向かっている」ということになります。

・予定のある未来：すでに決定されている（予定ができている）とき

・根拠がある未来：現在の状況から判断して近い未来に起こりそうなとき

4) 近接未来：be ~ing（〜することになっている）

I am working tomorrow.

動詞workが「be ~ing」で進行形になっています。I am working now. なら、「今、私は仕事をしているところです」となりますが、tomorrowなどの未来を表す副詞を伴うと、未来を表します。

・近接未来：(3)のbe going to よりもさらに計画や予定、根拠が具体的なとき

5) 予測＋近接未来：will be ~ing（〜することになるだろう）

I will be working tomorrow.

上記の（2）と（4）を足したもの。

6) 予定＋近接未来：be going to be ~ing（予定では〜することになっている）

I am going to be working tomorrow.

上記の（3）と（4）を足したもの。

▶注意：未来でも現在形

時（whenなど）や条件（ifなど）を表す副詞節では、未来のことであってもwillではなく現在時制を使います。時や条件が「実際に〜したら」の意味だからです。「実際のこと」は現在形で表し、「予測」のwillは使いません。

Exercises for the TOEIC® L&R Test

Part 5 Select the best answer to complete each sentence.

1. Today, in my presentation, I'm ______ to show you our new app for smartphones.
(A) have
(B) going
(C) will
(D) might

2. I ______ help you. Tell me how many handouts you need for the presentation tomorrow.
(A) am
(B) will
(C) going
(D) was

3. We will have to discuss it again when our boss ______ back from India.
(A) will come
(B) is going to come
(C) came
(D) comes

4. If you look at the graph, you ______ see there was a significant increase in the sales.
(A) will
(B) need to
(C) want
(D) are

5. According to the list, we ______ 32 people at the presentation tomorrow.
(A) had
(B) have to
(C) were having
(D) are having

Part 6 Select the best answer to complete the text.

To: Adam Collins
From: Bill Watson

Dear Adam,
It has been decided that we will soon be presenting our new braking system to Lloyd Motors. As you know, we have put a lot of time and effort into developing this product. Especially, the efforts of our R&D department have been remarkable. **–1–**. Based on your experience and achievements, I recommended you as a presenter to the manager. It **–2–** officially accepted yesterday. **–3–**, I would like to have a meeting with you as soon as possible to **–4–** this matter. Please let me know when you will be available next week.

1. (A) Unfortunately, his product is not so attractive.
(B) So, this presentation will be a very important one.
(C) I'll give them a free sample to try.
(D) In fact, I made them myself.

2. (A) is
(B) will be
(C) was
(D) has been

3. (A) So
(B) Because
(C) For example
(D) But

4. (A) say
(B) tell
(C) talk
(D) discuss

Part 7 Read the memo and attached document, and choose the best answer to each question.

To: John
From: Ken

As you requested, I am now preparing materials for our next presentation. I have just made a draft of the introduction to the presentation for you. Will you please read it (attached to this memo) and give me your feedback?

There is only one week left until the day of the presentation, so will you please reply ASAP? If this is OK, then I will start working on the rest.

Presentation Date: July 30
Time: 10:00-11:00 A.M.
Client: Index One Service Co. Ltd.

<SPEECH DRAFT>
Hello, everyone. I'm John Smith from the sales division of Mason Electric. Today, I would like to introduce our new product, the aromatic humidifier HMD-12. It is a humidifier with three functions: humidification, scent, and LED light. Ten LED lights and a mist create a fire that looks like a real one, creating a warm and romantic atmosphere like being by a warm fireplace. Now, I'd like to share with you the details with some demonstrations.

1. What is the purpose of the memo?
   (A) To give advice
   (B) To ask for comments
   (C) To schedule a meeting
   (D) To apologize

2. When is Ken most likely writing the memo?
   (A) July 9
   (B) July 16
   (C) July 23
   (D) July 30

3. Who is John?
   (A) An engineer
   (B) A shop manager
   (C) A client
   (D) A sales representative

4. What will Ken probably do when he gets a reply from John?
   (A) Leave a memo again
   (B) Call John
   (C) Meet John
   (D) Continue the preparation

5. What does this product NOT do?
   (A) Play romantic music
   (B) Produce fragrance
   (C) Humidify a room
   (D) Give off light

CHAPTER 9

現在完了形

Accommodation

本章での学習

▶文法：現在完了形の復習・確認
▶話題：Accommodation
▶演習：Part 5 → Part 1 → Part 2 → Part 3 → Part 4形式の問題演習

事前学習

① Vocabulary 9とGrammar 9の問題に解答し、「語彙・文法クイズ」に備える。
② Part 3の音声を聞き、ディクテーション(書き取り)をする。

語彙・文法クイズ

Vocabulary 1 ～ 9とGrammar 1 ～ 9から5問(日本語→英語)

Vocabulary 9

Audio① 74

1 ～ 10の語句を英語にしましょう。その後で音声を聞いて確認しましょう。

1. ホテルの部屋を予約する　＿＿＿＿＿＿ /book a hotel room
2. 同僚　＿＿＿＿＿＿
3. 保育園　＿＿＿＿＿＿ school
4. ～まで歩いて10分です。　It's a ten-minute ＿＿＿＿＿＿ to ～
5. 最優先事項　top ＿＿＿＿＿＿
6. ～することが許される　be ＿＿＿＿＿＿ to ～
7. 許可なしに　without ＿＿＿＿＿＿
8. 分譲マンション　＿＿＿＿＿＿
9. ゴミ捨て　＿＿＿＿＿＿ disposal
10. 規則に従う　follow ＿＿＿＿＿＿

Grammar 9

1 ～ 5の空所を埋めましょう。その後で、音声を聞いて確認しましょう。

1. もう宿題は終わりましたか。

   ＿＿＿＿＿ you finished your homework yet?

2. 沖縄には二度行ったことがあります。

   I have ＿＿＿＿＿ to Okinawa twice.

3. 私は学生証をなくしてしまいました（まだ、見つかっていません）

   I have ＿＿＿＿＿ my student ID.

4. あなたはジブリ映画を見たことはありますか。

   Have you ＿＿＿＿＿ seen a Ghibli movie?

5. どのくらい待っているのですか。

   How ＿＿＿＿＿ have you been waiting?

Pair Practice

・Vocabulary 9を、瞬時に「日本語→英語」にできるように、ペア（AとB）を組んで練習しましょう（1分間）。1分後にAとBの役割を交換し、同様に練習しましょう（1分間）。

A: 教科書を見ながらBに日本語を与える

B: 教科書を閉じたままAが与える日本語を英語にする

A: Bが即答できなければ、すぐにその英語を教え、1分間の内にどの語句もスラスラ英語で言えるようにさせる

・Grammar 9の例文についても同様の練習をしましょう（1分間）。

Grammar Review 9

現在完了形

	have (has)	+ 過去分詞		
	持っている	～したことを		
I	have	gained	two kilos.	
私は	持っている	増えたことを	2キロ	→(私は2キロ体重が増えた)

英語の時制で分かりにくいのが「現在完了」です。基本的な理解の仕方はhave（持っている）＋過去分詞（～したことを）でいいでしょう。「どうする」（動詞）の意味や ＋α（副詞）の意味などで、結果としては以下の3つのタイプに分類できます。空所を埋めながら確認・整理しましょう。

1) 完了・結果：（今）～した（状態にある）

The meeting has ＿＿＿＿＿ started.（ミーティングはちょうど始まったところです）

Has the meeting started ＿＿＿＿＿ ?（ミーティングはもう始まっていますか）

Yes, it has ＿＿＿＿＿＿ started.（はい、すでに始まっています）

No, it has not started ＿＿＿＿＿ .（いいえ、まだ始まっていません）

I have lost my smartphone.（私はスマホをなくしてしまった）

2) 経験：～したことがある

I have seen that movie ＿＿＿＿＿＿＿＿＿＿ .（あの映画は三度見たことがあります）

Have you ＿＿＿＿＿ been to America?（あなたはアメリカに行ったことがありますか）

I have ＿＿＿＿＿ eaten this much before.（今までこんなたくさん食べたことは一度もない）

3) 継続：ずっと～してきた

a) 状態の動詞

I have known her ＿＿＿＿＿＿ we were in elementary school.
（私は小学校の頃から彼女を知っています）

＿＿＿＿＿ long have you been in the IT business?
（あなたはIT業界にはどのくらい携わってきましたか）

b) 動作の動詞（現在完了進行形：have/has + been + ~ing）

I have been studying English ＿＿＿＿＿ seven years.
（私は英語を7年間ずっと勉強しています）

▶現在完了形

現在完了形は「今の状態」を表現します。ただし、have/has + 過去分詞 なので、「今、持っている」+「過去に起こったことを」といった状態を表します。

1) 完了・結果

The meeting has just started.
「ミーティングは／ちょうど始まった／を今持っている(そういう状態)」→ 始まったばかり

I have lost my smartphone.
「私は／スマホをなくした／を今持っている(そういう状態)」→ なくした(まだその状態)

2) 経験

I have seen that movie three times.
「私は／その映画を三度見た／を今持っている」→ 今まで見たことがある

3) 継続

I have known her since we were in elementary school.
「私は／小学校以来彼女を知っていた／を今持っている」→ ずっと知っている

▶過去形と現在完了形

① I lost my smartphone. (過去形)
② I have lost my smartphone. (現在完了形)

①のように過去形を使うと「私はスマホをなくした」と、単に過去にあった事実だけを述べることになります。今でもなくなったままかどうかについては分かりません。それに対して、②のように現在完了形を使うと「なくしたことを今もっている」、つまり、「(なくしてしまって) 今もなくした状態だ」を表すことになります。

また、現在完了形は「今の状態」を述べる表現であるため、I have lost my smartphone two days ago. のように過去を表す副詞(句)と一緒に使うことはありません。

Exercises for the TOEIC® L&R Test

Part 5 Select the best answer to complete each sentence.

1. Have you ______ a hotel room for your business trip to London yet?
   (A) had reserved
   (B) to reserve
   (C) reserved
   (D) reserving

2. ______ have you been working as a front desk clerk at this hotel?
   (A) How many
   (B) How long
   (C) How come
   (D) How about

3. I have ______ checked out because I need to take the 9:30 bus to the airport.
   (A) never
   (B) already
   (C) often
   (D) once

4. This is the most gorgeous hotel that I have ______ stayed at.
   (A) just
   (B) yet
   (C) twice
   (D) ever

5. I ________ breakfast from room service an hour ago but it has not been delivered yet.
   (A) ordered
   (B) have ordered
   (C) will order
   (D) am going to

Part 1 Listen and select the one statement that best describes what you see in the picture. **Audio① 76-78**

1.

Ⓐ Ⓑ Ⓒ Ⓓ

2.

Ⓐ Ⓑ Ⓒ Ⓓ

Part 2 Listen and select the best response to each question or statement. **Audio① 79-83**

1. Ⓐ Ⓑ Ⓒ **2.** Ⓐ Ⓑ Ⓒ **3.** Ⓐ Ⓑ Ⓒ **4.** Ⓐ Ⓑ Ⓒ

Part 3 Listen and select the best answer to each question. **Audio① 84-86**

1. Where is this conversation most likely taking place?
(A) At a real-estate agency
(B) At a nursery school
(C) At a station
(D) At a supermarket

2. How long does it take from the house to the station?
(A) 5 minutes (C) 15 minutes
(B) 10 minutes (D) 50 minutes

3. What does the woman mean when she says, "That's probably the top priority for me"?
(A) That's the least important thing for me.
(B) That's the most important thing for me.
(C) That's out of the question.
(D) That's the most difficult problem.

Part 4 Listen and select the best answer to each question. **Audio① 87-89**

1. What kind of announcement is this?
(A) Requests
(B) An advertisement
(C) An apology
(D) Sales

2. Who most likely are the listeners?
(A) Professional musicians
(B) The residents of the condominium
(C) Pet shop owners
(D) Garbage collectors

3. What are the listeners asked to do about garbage?
(A) To throw it at the entrance
(B) To sort it
(C) To collect it every day
(D) To recycle it

CHAPTER 10

前置詞

Public Facilities

本章での学習

▶文法：前置詞の復習・確認
▶話題：Public Facilities
▶演習：Part 5 → Part 6 → Part 7形式の問題演習

事前学習

① Vocabulary 10とGrammar 10の問題に解答し、「語彙・文法クイズ」に備える。
② Part 7の英文（1つ目）をチャンク単位で全文和訳をする。

語彙・文法クイズ

Vocabulary 1 ～ 10とGrammar 1 ～ 10から5問（日本語→英語）

Vocabulary 10

Audio① 90

1 ～ 10の語句を英語にしましょう。その後で音声を聞いて確認しましょう。

1. 改装計画	______________ project
2. 資金不足	lack of ______________
3. 市（自治体）の屋内プール	______________ indoor swimming pool
4. 市役所	city ______________
5. 公共施設	______________ facilities
6. 問い合わせありがとうございます。	Thank you for your ______________ .
7. 駐車場	______________ lot
8. 本の返却期限	due ______________ of a book
9. 10ドルの過料（罰金）を払う	pay a ______________ of $10
10. 購入価格	purchase ______________

Grammar 10

1 ～ 5の空所を埋めましょう。その後で、音声を聞いて確認しましょう。

1. その授業は9時45分に始まります。

   The class begins _________ 9:45.

2. 壁に貼ってあるカレンダーを見てください。

   Look at the calendar _________ the wall.

3. 彼女はそのレポートを3日で書き終えた。

   She finished the paper _________ three days.

4. これはあなたへのプレゼントです。

   This is a present _________ you.

5. 彼は朝から晩まで働いた。

   He worked from morning _________ night.

Pair Practice

・Vocabulary 10を、瞬時に「日本語→英語」にできるように、ペア(AとB)を組んで練習しましょう(1分間)。1分後にAとBの役割を交換し、同様に練習しましょう(1分間)。

A: 教科書を見ながらBに日本語を与える

B: 教科書を閉じたままAが与える日本語を英語にする

A: Bが即答できなければ、すぐにその英語を教え、1分間の内にどの語句もスラスラ英語で言えるようにさせる

・Grammar 10の例文についても同様の練習をしましょう(1分間)。

Grammar Review 10

前置詞

前置詞 ＋ 名詞

英語の前置詞はどうにもやっかいです。catなら「猫」と覚えればそれで済みますが、例えば前置詞のatの訳はというと「～を」「～に」「～で」のようにつかみどころがありません。ポイントは、それぞれの「核」となるイメージをつかむことです。代表的な前置詞について、空所を埋めながら、確認・整理しましょう。

前置詞：イメージ	例　文
1) on：接着 (～の上に) (～について)	There are some books **on** the desk. (机の上に何冊か本があります) There is a fly **on** the ceiling. (天井にハエがいます) We had a discussion ______ SDGs. (私たちはSDGsについて話し合った)
2) in：範囲 (～の中で) (～の時間で)	Our head office is **in** Nagoya. (本社は名古屋にあります) I'll be back ______ ten minutes. (10分で戻ります)
3) at：1点を指す矢印	She smiled ______ me. (彼女は私にほほ笑んだ) The meeting begins **at** 10:00. (ミーティングは10時に始まります)
4) to： 到着点に届く矢印 from：起点	We took a Shinkansen ______ Tokyo ______ Osaka. (私たちは東京から大阪まで新幹線で行った)
5) for：幅のある矢印 (～に対して)	Take the train ______ Shinjuku and get off at the third station. (新宿方面の電車に乗り、3つ目の駅で降りてください) Thank you **for** coming. (来てくれてありがとう)
6) of：分離 (～の) (～から)	I like the paintings **of** Picasso. (私はピカソの絵が好きです) He is independent ______ his parents. (彼は親から自立しています)

7) with：付帯／関係 (～と) (～に関して)	I went to see a movie **with** Ayaka. (私は綾香と映画を見に行った) Is it OK ________ you? (あなたに関してはそれでOKですか)
8) into： 外から中へ／ 変化	We all walked **into** the meeting room. (私たちは皆、会議室に入って行った) Can you translate this ________ English? (これを英語に訳せますか)
9) through：貫通	The train went **through** the tunnel. (列車はトンネルを通り抜けた)
10) among： 3者以上の間	His songs are popular **among** young people. (彼の歌は若者の間で人気がある)

▶前置詞：物理的な意味 → 抽象的な意味

① There are some books **on** the desk.（物理的な意味）

② We had a discussion **on** SDGs.（抽象的な意味）

①のように、前置詞が場所や位置関係などの物理的な意味を表すのに使われていることはよく分かりますね。実は、この物理的な意味が発展して、②のように抽象的な意味も表します。この抽象的な意味が、前置詞を難しくしている理由です。

この解決策は「イメージ」です。例に上げたonという前置詞は「接着」という物理的な「核」になる意味があります。この「接着」のイメージから抽象的な意味を連想します。a discussion on SDGsは「SDGsに接着した話し合い」→「SDGsについての話し合い」のように。

▶重要な前置詞

前ページの表の中で特に重要な1)～7)について説明を加えます。

1) on：接着

onについては上記の説明の通りです。2つ目の例文、There is a fly **on** the ceiling. も「接着」のイメージから「天井にハエがいます」は理解できますね。

2) in：範囲

Our head office is **in** Nagoya. は「範囲」ですんなり理解できますが、2つ目のI'll be back **in** ten minutes. はやや複雑です。考え方は「時間が進む範囲」、つまり「10分が進む範囲で」→「10分で」。

3) at：一点を指す矢印

She smiled **at** me. は「彼女」から「私」への視線が矢印でイメージできます。The meeting begins **at** 10:00.では「時点」を示す「時計の針」がイメージできます。

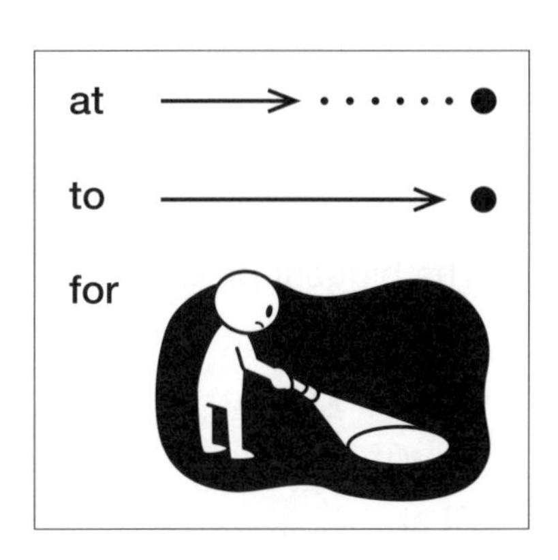

4) to：到着点に届く矢印

We took a Shinkansen train from Tokyo **to** Osaka. これは「到着点の大阪」までの矢印のイメージです。

5) for：幅のある矢印(懐中電灯の光)

矢印で厄介なのがこのforです。Take the train **for** Shinjuku ... から、電車が新宿という「一点」でも「到着点」でもなく、新宿の方に向かっているイメージです。Thank you **for** coming. については、「感謝する」対象をスポットライトで照らしているイメージです。「～に対して」と解釈しましょう。

6) of：分離

ofについては、I like the paintings **of** Picasso. のように、ほとんどは「～の」で対処できます。しかし、中には2つ目の例文、He is independent **of** his parents. のよう「～の」では意味をなさないものがあります。ofの「核」となる意味は「分離」です。「～から離れる」というイメージです。「～の」で意味をなさなければ、「～から」と「分離」のイメージで解釈しましょう。

7) with：付帯・関係

I went to see a movie **with** Ayaka. は「付帯」から「彩香と一緒に」と容易に理解できます。問題は2つ目の Is it OK **with** you? です。このwithは「付帯」が発展して「関係」を表すものです。「～に関して」と解釈します。実はこの意味で使われているwithは少なくありません。

Exercises for the TOEIC® L&R Test

Part 5 Select the best answer to complete each sentence.

1. Go down this street for two blocks and turn right. You will see the post office _______ the right.
   (A) in
   (B) at
   (C) on
   (D) from

2. There are two restaurants, Chinese and Italian, and a cafe _______ the park.
   (A) to
   (B) through
   (C) among
   (D) in

3. The biggest problem _______ the renovation project of the library is a lack of funding.
   (A) among
   (B) with
   (C) at
   (D) to

4. The municipal indoor swimming pool is open _______ 10:00 A.M. until 9:00 P.M.
   (A) from
   (B) with
   (C) on
   (D) at

5. At the city hall on July 12, there is going to be a lecture _______ "How to Prevent Heatstroke."
   (A) to
   (B) in
   (C) at
   (D) on

Part 6 Select the best answer to complete the text.

What are "public facilities"? They are the facilities around us that anyone can **–1–** use as long as they follow the rules. These facilities are **–2–** with the money from taxes that people pay to their cities and towns. They include facilities that are useful **–3–** daily life like libraries and hospitals. Places like museums and parks where people can enjoy their time are also called "public facilities." **–4–**.

1. (A) freely
(B) hardly
(C) shortly
(D) unfortunately

2. (A) build
(B) built
(C) building
(D) to build

3. (A) on
(B) in
(C) at
(D) of

4. (A) So, many public facilities are closed down every year.
(B) You need special permission to use public facilities.
(C) As you can see, there are many different types of public facilities.
(D) Most of them are not useful for citizens.

Part 7 Read the e-mails and Web site and choose the best answer to each question.

To: Central Library
From: Fred Baker
Date: July 31
Subject: Late return

Dear Sir or Madam,

I borrowed a book from you two weeks ago on July 17. The return date is tomorrow, August 1, but I can't find it. I looked everywhere, but I'm afraid I seem to have lost it. Are there any penalties for a lost book? What if I can find it later?

Best regards,
Fred Baker

To: Fred Baker
From: Sue Holland
Date: July 31
Subject: Re: Late return

Dear Mr. Baker,

Thank you for your inquiry.

Please visit our website for the policy on late returns and lost books.
Here's the information about the book you borrowed.
Title: Tomorrow's World
Author: Max Smith
Publication date: February 14, 2018
Price: $ 35

Yours sincerely,
Sue Holland

Location: 4 North Street, Greenville
Phone: 005-1234-5678
Opening hours: 9:00 A.M. to 9:00 P.M. on weekdays
9:00 A.M. to 6:00 P.M. on weekends and holidays
Access: 5-minute walk from the north exit of Greenville Station

*There is no parking lot.
*The children's book section on the second floor is open until 5 P.M. on weekdays.
*The book drop is located by the library entrance, available 24/7.
For more information, please click the link below.
https://centrallibrary.greenville.com/borrowbooks

Policy for Late Return & Lost Book Penalty

You must return the book you borrowed by the due date. You are not charged for late returns. However, books returned more than 30 days after the due date will be considered lost. In that case, you must pay the purchase price of the book.

1. How much fine does Mr. Baker have to pay if he cannot find the book before August 31?
(A) $30 (B) $35 (C) $45 (D) no fine

2. When is the scheduled return date for the book?
(A) February 14 (B) July 17 (C) July 31 (D) August 1

3. How far is the library from the nearest station?
(A) 5 minutes on foot
(B) 5 minutes by bicycle
(C) 5 minutes by bus
(D) 5 minutes by car

4. How long is the library open on Sundays?
(A) Six hours
(B) Nine hours
(C) 12 hours
(D) 24 hours

5. Where is the children's book section?
(A) 1st floor
(B) 2nd floor
(C) 3rd floor
(D) 4th floor

CHAPTER 11

不定詞

Appointments

本章での学習

▶文法：不定詞の復習・確認
▶話題：Appointments
▶演習：Part 5 → Part 1 → Part 2 → Part 3 → Part 4形式の問題演習

事前学習

① Vocabulary 11とGrammar 11の問題に解答し、「語彙・文法クイズ」に備える。
② Part 3の音声を聞き、ディクテーション(書き取り)をする。

語彙・文法クイズ

Vocabulary 1 ～ 11とGrammar 1 ～ 11から5問(日本語→英語)

Vocabulary 11

Audio② 01

1 ～ 10の語句を英語にしましょう。その後で音声を聞いて確認しましょう。

1. 金曜日に会うアポを設定する　　________ an appointment for Friday
2. あなたは金曜日に都合がつきますか。　　Are you ________ on Friday?
3. スケジュールを変更する　　________
4. 金曜日は都合がいいですか。　　Is Friday ________ for you?
5. ミーティングに参加する　　________ a meeting
6. 直接あなたと話す　　talk to you in ________
7. 対面であなたと話す　　talk to you face to ________
8. オンラインであなたと話す　　talk to you ________
9. …をあなたに知らせる　　________ you that ...
10. 出張中で(こちらにはいない)　　be ________ of town

Grammar 11

Audio② 02

1～5の空所を埋めましょう。その後で、音声を聞いて確認しましょう。

1. 私は弁護士になるために法律を勉強しています。
   I'm studying law ________ be a lawyer.

2. 今日終えなければならないレポートがあります。
   I have a paper to __________ today.

3. あなたとまた会えて嬉しいです。
   I am ________ to see you again.

4. それを私が一人でやるのは難しいです。
   It is difficult ________ me to do it by myself.

5. 図書館では音を立てないようにしてください。
   Try ________ to make any noise in the library.

Pair Practice

・Vocabulary 11を、瞬時に「日本語→英語」にできるように、ペア(AとB)を組んで練習しましょう(1分間)。1分後にAとBの役割を交換し、同様に練習しましょう(1分間)。

A: 教科書を見ながらBに日本語を与える

B: 教科書を閉じたままAが与える日本語を英語にする

A: Bが即答できなければ、すぐにその英語を教え、1分間の内にどの語句もスラスラ英語で言えるようにさせる

・Grammar 11の例文についても同様の練習をしましょう(1分間)。

Grammar Review 11

不定詞

to + 動詞の原形

「to + 動詞の原形」のことを「不定詞」と呼びます。3つの用法があり、訳し方もいくつかあります。例文で特徴（特に位置）を押さえながら確認・整理しましょう。

1. 不定詞の用法	例文	位置
1) 名詞的用法 「〜すること」	I want _____ join a fitness club. （私はフィットネスクラブに入会したい）	動詞の後 主語
2) 形容的用法 「〜すべき…」	There are two items _____ discuss today. （今日は話し合うことが2項目あります）	名詞の後
3) 副詞的用法 目的： 「〜するために」	We'll meet tomorrow _____ decide the budget. （私たちは明日、予算を決めるため会議をします）	文末 文頭
副詞的用法 原因：「〜して」	I'm very pleased _____ meet you. （お会いできてとても嬉しいです）	感情表現 の後
副詞的用法 根拠：「〜するとは」	He must be careless _____ make such a mistake. （そんなミスをするとは、彼は不注意な人に違いない）	判断を下す 表現の後
副詞的用法 形容詞修飾： 「〜するのに…」	The target is not easy _____ achieve. （その目標は達成するのに容易ではありません）	形容詞の後

2. 不定詞と形式主語・目的語のit	
1) It is ... to ~ 「〜することは…だ」	**It** is easy _____ answer the question. （彼を説得することは簡単だ）
2) It is ... for △ to ~ 「△が〜することは…だ」	_____ is not easy _____ me _____ answer the question. （私が彼を説得することは簡単ではない）
3) It is ... of △ to ~ 「△が〜するとは…だ」	**It** is kind _____ you _____ help me. （手伝ってくれるなんて、あなたは親切ですね） 注意：…に人の性格・性質を表す語（kind, nice, clever, carelessなど）が来る場合
4) S V it ... to ~ 「Sは〜することが…だとVする」	I found _____ difficult **to** answer the question. （彼を説得するのは難しいとわかった）

3. 不定詞の否定形と完了形	例 文
1) 不定詞の否定形 not to ~	Be careful _____ to catch a cold. (かぜを引かないように気をつけて)
2) 不定詞の完了形 to have + 過去分詞	She seems **to** have been busy yesterday. (彼女は、昨日は忙しかったようだ)

4. 動詞と不定詞の組み合わせ	例 文
SVO + to ~ 「SはOに～することをVする」	I asked her _____ help me. (私は彼女に私を手伝ってくれるようにお願いした)

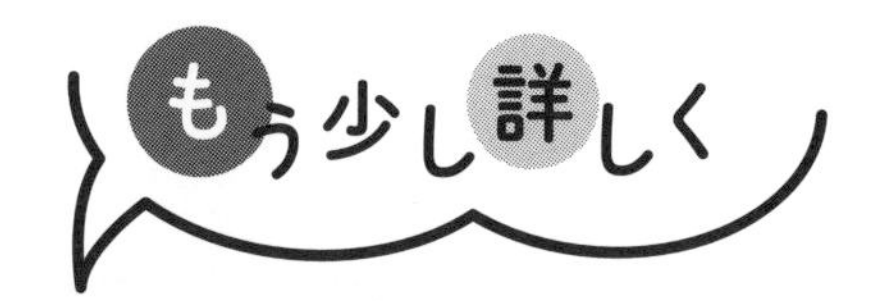

▶不定詞

① I want to play tennis tomorrow.
② I enjoyed playing tennis yesterday.

不定詞(to + 動詞の原形)のtoは、もともと「矢印」を表す前置詞(Grammar Review 10)なので、「(実際に)～していること」ではなく、①のように「(これから)～すること」、あるいは「(頭で考えている)～すること」を意味します。これが不定詞の基本的な意味です。なお、「(実際に)～していること」は、②のように「動詞-ing」(動名詞)で表現されます。

1. 不定詞の用法

表にあるように、不定詞には大きく3つ、細かくは6つの用法(意味)があります。文中でどれを意味するかは、「基本文型」(Grammar Review 1)と「名詞の修飾」(Grammar Review 2)の2つのルールと、表に示した「不定詞の位置」からほぼ見当がつきます。文の構造とその文の中での不定詞の位置に注意しながら、適切な意味をつかみましょう。

2. 不定詞と形式主語・目的語のit

① To persuade him is easy.
② It is easy to persuade him. (形式主語)
(それは簡単だ:それ=彼を説得すること)

③ I found to persuade him difficult. 〈注意:実際にはこのような文はありません〉
④ I found it difficult to persuade him. (形式目的語)
(私はそれを難しいと思った:それ=彼を説得すること)

①の文をitを使って書き換えたのが②の文で、③の文を書き変えたのが④の文です。②と④は、形式的に「それ」と先に言っておき、後ろに不定詞を従えて、「それ」って何かと言うと「～すること」のように説明する構文です。

3. 不定詞の完了形

① It seems that she was busy yesterday.
② She seems to have been busy yesterday.

①の文を、sheを主語にして書き換えたものが②の文です。seem to have ~（過去分詞）で「～したように思われる」。

4. 動詞と不定詞の組み合わせ(SVO + to ~)：「SはOに～することをVする」

I	asked	her	to help me.
(私は	お願いした	彼女に	私を手伝うことを)

こうした形を取る動詞はaskの他にwant, tell, advise, allowなど少なくありません。たくさん英文を読みながら慣れていきましょう。

Exercises for the TOEIC® L&R Test

Part 5 Select the best answer to complete each sentence.

1. Ms. Robert sent an e-mail to her client _______ when he can meet her.
(A) has asked
(B) asked
(C) to have asked
(D) to ask

2. Hurry up. Our appointment with Mr. Brown is at 3:30. There is _______ to lose.
(A) no one
(B) no time
(C) nothing
(D) nobody

3. Wednesday from 3:00 sounds good to us. That gives us _______ time to prepare.
(A) many
(B) no
(C) enough
(D) little

4. It was careless _______ you to arrange two appointments at the same time on the same day.
(A) for
(B) to
(C) with
(D) of

5. The meeting last Friday seems to _______ successful. I got a good response from the client today.
(A) have been
(B) be
(C) was
(D) is

Part 1 Listen and select the one statement that best describes what you see in the picture. Audio② 03-05

1.

Ⓐ Ⓑ Ⓒ Ⓓ

2.

Ⓐ Ⓑ Ⓒ Ⓓ

Part 2 Listen and select the best response to each question or statement. Audio② 06-10

1. Ⓐ Ⓑ Ⓒ   2. Ⓐ Ⓑ Ⓒ   3. Ⓐ Ⓑ Ⓒ   4. Ⓐ Ⓑ Ⓒ

Part 3 Listen and select the best answer to each question. Audio② 11-13

1. When did Greg last visit the head office?
   (A) A year ago
   (B) Two years ago
   (C) Three years ago
   (D) Four years ago

2. What does the woman mean when she says, "I was hoping to talk to you in person"?
   (A) She wants to send e-mail to Greg.
   (B) She wants to meet Greg face to face.
   (C) She wants to discuss things with Greg on the phone.
   (D) She wants to discuss things with Greg online.

3. How long is Greg going to stay in Chicago?
   (A) One day
   (B) Two days
   (C) Three days
   (D) Four days

Part 4 Listen and select the best answer to each question. 

1. Where does the speaker work?
(A) At a clinic
(B) At a factory
(C) At an insurance company
(D) At a department store

2. Why isn't Dr. Jason available?
(A) He's very busy.
(B) He doesn't feel well.
(C) He's attending a conference.
(D) He's taking a vacation.

3. What does the speaker imply when she says, "I apologize for the inconvenience"?
(A) She is sorry that she could not change the schedule.
(B) She is sorry that she had to change the schedule.
(C) She is happy that she changed the schedule.
(D) She is happy that she didn't change the schedule.

CHAPTER 12

仮定法過去

Meetings

本章での学習

▶文法：仮定法過去の復習・確認
▶話題：Meetings
▶演習：Part 5 → Part 6 → Part 7形式の問題演習

事前学習

①Vocabulary 12とGrammar 12の問題に解答し、「語彙・文法クイズ」に備える。
②Part 7の英文（1つ目）をチャンク単位で全文和訳をする。

語彙・文法クイズ

Vocabulary 1～12とGrammar 1～12から5問（日本語→英語）

Vocabulary 12

Audio② 17

1～10の語句を英語にしましょう。その後で音声を聞いて確認しましょう。

1.	私は～で手がふさがっている	I'm tied up ___________ ～
2.	10分間の休憩を取る	___________ a ten-minute break
3.	提案を出す	___________ forward suggestions
4.	いいアイディアを思いついた。	A good idea came to my _______________ .
5.	定期的に	on a _______________ basis
6.	次回のプレゼン	_________________ presentation
7.	会うのが早ければ早いほどよい。	The _______________ we meet, the better.
8.	添付書類	attached _________________
9.	もし可能であれば	if _________________
10.	～に関しては	_________ for ～

Grammar 12

1～5の空所を埋めましょう。その後で、音声を聞いて確認しましょう。

1. もし私があなただったら、彼のプロポーズを受けるでしょう。
   If I were you, I ___________ accept his proposal.

2. 鳥のように空を飛べたらいいのになあ。
   I wish I ___________ fly in the sky like a bird.

3. 彼は彼女についてあたかも何でも知っているかのように話す。
   He talks as _________ he knew everything about her.

4. まだ起きてるの？もう寝てもいい時間よ。
   Are you still up? It's about time you _________ to bed.

5. 沖縄に行きたいけど、お金がたくさんかかるだろうなあ。
   I want to go to Okinawa, but it ___________ cost a lot of money.

Pair Practice

・Vocabulary 12を、瞬時に「日本語→英語」にできるように、ペア（AとB）を組んで練習しましょう（1分間）。1分後にAとBの役割を交換し、同様に練習しましょう（1分間）。

A: 教科書を見ながらBに日本語を与える

B: 教科書を閉じたままAが与える日本語を英語にする

A: Bが即答できなければ、すぐにその英語を教え、1分間の内にどの語句もスラスラ英語で言えるようにさせる

・Grammar 12の例文についても同様の練習をしましょう（1分間）。

Grammar Review 12

仮定法過去

If	I	knew	it,	I	would tell	you.
If	何が ＋	どうした(過去) ＋	…,	何は ＋	助動詞(過去) ～ ＋	….

英語で「仮の話」をするときには「仮定法過去」と「仮定法過去完了」(Grammar Review 13) という表現手法があります。「仮定法過去」が「今に対する仮定」に対して、「仮定法過去完了」は「あのときの仮定」です。ここでは「仮定法過去」について、空所を埋めながら整理・確認していきましょう。

基本パターン

If 何が+どうした…, 何は +
- would ～ (～するだろう)
- could ～ (～できるだろう、～する可能性があるだろう)
- might ～ (ひょっとして～するかもしれない)
- should ～ (～すべきだ、～するはずだ)

If I ________ it, I would tell you.
(知っていたら、あなたに話すだろう)
If I had time, I ________ go with you.
(時間があったら、あなたと一緒に行けるんだが)

応用パターン

1. wishを使ったもの	I wish 何が ＋ ～ (過去) … (何が～だったらいいのになあ)
	I **wish** I ________ a good singer. (歌がうまかったらいいのになあと思う) I **wish** I ________ speak English well. (英語が上手に話せたらいいのになあと思う)
2. as ifを使ったもの	as if 何が ＋ ～ (過去) … (まるで 何が～かのように)
	He speaks **as if** he ________ everything. (彼は話す／まるで何でも知っているかのように) 注意: as if ... の中を過去にせずに現在(直説法)で表現することも少なくない。
3. It is time を使ったもの	It is time 何が ＋ ～ (過去) … (もう何が～していていい頃だ)
	It is about time you ________ job hunting. (もう就職活動を始めていてもいい頃だ)
4. If節が不在のもの	A: How about meeting at 6:30? (6時半に会うのはどう？) B: That **would** be fine. (それでいいでしょう) 注意: If節がない場合は、文脈から「もし…だったら」という含みを感じ取って解釈する。

▶仮定法過去：「仮の話」

If I **knew** it, I **would** tell you.

「仮に…だったら、…するだろう」と表現したいときには、動詞や助動詞を過去形にして表現します。とは言っても、ただ過去形にするだけでは、ただの過去の話になってしまいます。「仮の話」をするときには、表で示したようなパターンで過去形を使うときに限られます。基本パターンと応用パターンをしっかり覚えておきましょう。

▶If節が不在のパターン（表の応用パターンの４）

A: How about meeting at 6:30?
B: That **would** be fine.

この会話のように、過去の話ではないのに、なぜ突然wouldのような過去形が出てくるのだろう、と疑問に思ったことはありませんか。これは、Chapter 6のGrammar Review（助動詞）で述べた「仮定法過去で使われるcould, might, would, should」で、表の応用パターンの４にあたります。基本パターンのIf S+V（過去形）…（もし…だったら）が省略されていると考え、「もし…だったら」の含みを加えて解釈します。この含みは文脈から感じ取ります。下の文で試してみましょう。

① I have another engagement. Otherwise, I **could** stay longer and have more talk with you.
（別の約束があります。そうでもなければ、もう少し長くいてもっとお話ができるのですが）

② A person with common sense **would** not say such a thing.
（常識のある人ならそんなことは言わないだろう）

③ I think your idea is great, but **could** it work in practice?
（アイディアは素晴らしいと思うけど、実際にうまく行くだろうか）

④ **Could** you help me? I **could** finish the work easily with your help.
（手伝って頂けますか。あなたの助けがあれば簡単にその仕事を終えることができるのですが）

Exercises for the TOEIC® L&R Test

Part 5 Select the best answer to complete each sentence.

1. I ________ join the meeting if it were in the morning. I'm tied up with other things all afternoon.
(A) will
(B) could
(C) on
(D) from

2. It's about time we ________ on to the next topic. We still have four items to discuss today.
(A) moves
(B) will move
(C) moving
(D) moved

3. If we ______ a little more budget, we could spend more on TV commercials.
(A) are having
(B) had
(C) will have
(D) have to

4. I think your plan is great, ______ do you think the manager will accept it?
(A) but
(B) if
(C) and
(D) or

5. Would you like to take a ten-minute break now, or would you ______ continue?
(A) better
(B) like
(C) want
(D) rather

Part 6 Select the best answer to complete the text.

There are many types of meetings. **–1–**, a kickoff meeting is a meeting at the beginning of a project. In this meeting, you talk about the project's objectives, schedule, budget, and so on. **–2–**. In this type of meeting, you put forward as many ideas and suggestions as you can think of. The good thing about this meeting is you can feel free to say anything that comes to your mind. There are also meetings that you have on a regular **–3–**. In these meetings, you meet daily, weekly, or monthly to share information and discuss problems. Whatever the type of meeting, to understand its purpose clearly is the key **–4–** making it an efficient one.

1. (A) Also
   (B) By the way
   (C) However
   (D) For example

2. (A) Another type of meeting is called a brainstorming meeting.
   (B) Schedule management is very important.
   (C) Teleconferencing has many disadvantages.
   (D) You can join meetings online from anywhere.

3. (A) member
   (B) time
   (C) basis
   (D) position

4. (A) to
   (B) of
   (C) in
   (D) at

Part 7 Read the e-mails and choose the best answer to each question.

To: Peter
From: Richard
Date: Thursday, October 5
Subject: Upcoming presentation

Hi Peter,

Our presentation is now only three weeks away. I think it's about time we discussed the details. When shall we meet? I am available on Thursday and Friday next week. What's your schedule? This is a very important presentation and there is a lot to talk about. So, I think the sooner we meet, the better.

Things I'd like to discuss are listed in the attached document, so read through it in advance. Please let me know if you have any suggestions.

Best regards,

Richard

To: Richard
From: Peter
Date: Friday, October 6
Subject: Re: Upcoming presentation

Hi Richard,

Thanks for your e-mail.

I was just thinking that we should have a meeting soon, too. I am available on Thursday next week. If possible, the afternoon would be more convenient for me, so how about meeting at 1:00? I'm available all afternoon until 5:00.

As for the attached document, for some reason, I cannot open it. Could you send it again when you reply?

Best,

Peter

1. What is the purpose of the first e-mail?
   (A) To arrange a meeting
   (B) To postpone a meeting
   (C) To cancel a meeting
   (D) To rearrange a meeting

2. Which days are good for Richard next week?
   (A) Sunday and Monday
   (B) Monday and Tuesday
   (C) Tuesday and Wednesday
   (D) Thursday and Friday

3. In the first e-mail, the words “in advance” in paragraph 2, line 2, is closest in meaning to
   (A) afterwards
   (B) beforehand
   (C) later
   (D) at the same time

4. When will the meeting most likely take place?
   (A) October 5
   (B) October 6
   (C) October 12
   (D) October 25

5. What does Peter ask Richard to do?
   (A) To open an attached document
   (B) To read an attached document
   (C) To delete an attached document
   (D) To resend an attached document

CHAPTER 13

仮定法過去完了

On the Street

本章での学習

▶文法：仮定法過去完了の復習・確認
▶話題：On the Street
▶演習：Part 5 → Part 1 → Part 2 → Part 3 → Part 4形式の問題演習

事前学習

① Vocabulary 13とGrammar 13の問題に解答し、「語彙・文法クイズ」に備える。
② Part 3の音声を聞き、ディクテーション(書き取り)をする。

語彙・文法クイズ

Vocabulary 1 ～ 13とGrammar 1 ～ 13から5問(日本語→英語)

Vocabulary 13

Audio② 19

1 ～ 10の語句を英語にしましょう。その後で音声を聞いて確認しましょう。

1. 事故に巻き込まれる	be ______________ in an accident
2. 道に迷う	be ___________
3. 営業日	______________ days
4. 通りの屋台	_____________ on the street
5. 食料品店	______________ store
6. たまには気分転換に	for a ______________
7. 偶然、魅力的な神社を見つける	find an attractive shrine by ______________
8. 今朝収穫された野菜	vegetables ______________ this morning
9. 10年間	for a ______________
10. 先日	the _____________ day

Grammar 13

1～5の空所を埋めましょう。その後で、音声を聞いて確認しましょう。

1. (あのとき)私のアドバイスを聞いていたら、あなたは成功していたでしょう。
   If you ________ taken my advice, you would have succeeded.

2. (あのとき)パーティーに来ていたら、あなたは彼に会うことができただろう。
   If you had come to the party, you ________ have met him.

3. (あのとき)あなたが一緒に来られたらよかったのになあ。
   I ________ you could have come with me.

4. 彼女はまるで幽霊でも見たかのような顔をしていた。
   She looked ________ if she had seen a ghost.

5. 彼の話は本当だった可能性がある(本当だったのかもしれない)。
   His story ________ have been true.

Pair Practice

・Vocabulary 13を、瞬時に「日本語→英語」にできるように、ペア(AとB)を組んで練習しましょう(1分間)。1分後にAとBの役割を交換し、同様に練習しましょう(1分間)。

A: 教科書を見ながらBに日本語を与える

B: 教科書を閉じたままAが与える日本語を英語にする

A: Bが即答できなければ、すぐにその英語を教え、1分間の内にどの語句もスラスラ英語で言えるようにさせる

・Grammar 13の例文についても同様の練習をしましょう(1分間)。

Grammar Review 13

仮定法過去完了

If I	had known it,	I	would	have told	you.
If 何が	**+どうした(過去完了)…,**	**何は**	**+ 助動詞(過去)**	**have ～ (過去分詞)**	**….**

英語で「あのとき」(過去)における「仮の話」をするときには「仮定法過去完了」という表現手法を使います。「仮定法過去」が「今に対する仮定」に対して、「仮定法過去完了」は「あのときの仮定」です。if節の中の動詞部分は過去完了 (**had +過去分詞**) に、また、帰結節の中の動詞部分は **助動詞の過去 + have+過去分詞** になります。空所を埋めながら確認・整理しましょう。

基本パターン
If 何が+ had+過去分詞…, 何は + { would have +過去分詞(～しただろう) / could have+過去分詞(～できただろう、可能性があっただろう) / might have+過去分詞(ひょっとして～したかもしれない) / should have+過去分詞(～すべきだった、～したはずだ) }
If I **had known** it, I **would have** ________ you. (もし(あのとき)知っていたら、あなたに話していただろう) If I **had had** time, I ________ **have gone** with you. (もし(あのとき)時間があったら、あなたと一緒に行けただろう)

応用パターン	
1. wishを使ったもの	I wish 何が ＋ ～ (過去完了) … (～だったらよかったのになあ) I **wish** I ________ **studied** harder. ((あのとき)もっと勉強しておけばよかったのになあと思う) I **wish** she **had told** me about it. ((あのとき)彼女がそのことを私に話してくれていたらよかったのにと思う)
2. as ifを使ったもの	as if 何が ＋ ～ (過去完了) … (まるで～だったかのように) She speaks **as if** she ________ **lived** in Paris. (彼女はまるで自分がパリに住んでいたかのように話す)
3. If節が不在	You ________ **have called** me. ((あのとき)私に電話をくれたらよかったのに)

注意：仮定法過去完了を仮定法過去とはっきり区別して感じ取るには、心の中で「あのとき」を加えて解釈するとよい。

▶仮定法過去完了：「(あのときの)仮の話」

If I **had known** it, I **would have told** you.

「仮に（あのとき）…だったら、…しただろう」と表現したいときには、動詞の部分を過去完了形にして表現します。仮定法過去と同様に、「仮の話」を表現するには、表で示したようなパターンで過去完了形を使うときに限られます。基本パターンと応用パターンをしっかり覚えておきましょう。

▶仮定法過去完了＋仮定法過去

If I **had finished** my homework yesterday, I **could** relax all day today.
もし昨日宿題を終えていたら、　　　　　　　今日は一日中のんびり過ごせるのだが。

このようなこともあります。「仮に（あのとき）…だったら、（今）…だろう」という表現です。前半のif節は「あのとき」で、後半の帰結節は「今」なので、「If節（過去完了）, 帰結節（過去）」という組み合わせになります。

▶If節が不在のパターン（表の応用パターンの3）

A: I was caught in a shower last night on my way home from the station.
B: Didn't you have an umbrella?
A: No. I got wet to the skin.
B: You **should have called** me. I **would have gone** to pick you up.

この会話のように、If節がなく突然「should have 過去分詞」や「would have 過去分詞」が出てくることがあります。これは、表の応用パターンの3です。基本パターンのIf節が省略されていると考え、「もし（あのとき）…だったら」の含みを加えて解釈します。この含みは、下に示したように文脈から感じ取ります。

① You **should have called** me.
(もしそんな状況だったら)私に電話をしてくれたらよかったのに。

注意：shouldはGrammar Review 6で説明したように「強制力」の弱い助動詞です。「〜すべきだ」というよりも「〜するとよい」に近いので、should have 過去分詞は「〜すればよかった」のような訳になります。

② I **would have gone** to pick you up.
(もしあのときそうしてくれてたら)車で迎えに行っただろう。

文脈から仮定の含みがはっきりしないときには、「何だったら、何であれば」のような言葉を加えるとよいかもしれません。①は「(何だったら) 電話をしてくれればよかったのに」、②は「(何だったら)車で迎えに行っただろう」のようになります。

Exercises for the TOEIC® L&R Test

Part 5 Select the best answer to complete each sentence.

1. If you had been more careful, you would not _______ been involved in the car accident.
(A) has
(B) have
(C) had
(D) having

2. If my phone _______ had the navigation app, I would have been lost on the way.
(A) had
(B) didn't have
(C) have
(D) hadn't

3. The street band in Shinjuku last night was great. I felt _______ I had been in New York.
(A) that
(B) as if
(C) when
(D) if

4. Twenty years ago we could have _______ more fancy cafes and restaurants on this street.
(A) to see
(B) be seeing
(C) saw
(D) seen

5. Perhaps I _______ have taken the other road. It might have been much quicker.
(A) should
(B) had
(C) will
(D) can

Part 1 Listen and select the one statement that best describes what you see in the picture. Audio② 21-23

1.

Ⓐ Ⓑ Ⓒ Ⓓ

2.

Ⓐ Ⓑ Ⓒ Ⓓ

Part 2 Listen and select the best response to each question or statement. Audio② 24-28

1. Ⓐ Ⓑ Ⓒ　2. Ⓐ Ⓑ Ⓒ　3. Ⓐ Ⓑ Ⓒ　4. Ⓐ Ⓑ Ⓒ

Part 3 Listen and select the best answer to each question. Audio② 29-31

1. Where are they talking?
   (A) On the street
   (B) In a supermarket
   (C) In a restaurant
   (D) At a grocery store

2. How much does the woman pay?
   (A) One dollar
   (B) Two dollars
   (C) Three dollars
   (D) Four dollars

3. When did the man start his business here?
   (A) One year ago
   (B) Two years ago
   (C) Three years ago
   (D) Four years ago

Part 4 Listen and select the best answer to each question. **Audio② 32-34**

1. What does the speaker enjoy doing daily?
(A) Taking photos
(B) Taking a walk in the morning
(C) Visiting shrines
(D) Working near his house

2. What did the speaker find the other day?
(A) A church
(B) A shrine
(C) A temple
(D) A cafe

3. How long has the speaker been living in this town?
(A) One year
(B) Five years
(C) Ten years
(D) Twenty years

CHAPTER 14

動名詞と分詞構文

Vacation

本章での学習

▶文法：動名詞・分詞構文の復習・確認
▶話題：Vacation
▶演習：Part 5 → Part 6 → Part 7形式の問題演習

事前学習

① Vocabulary 14とGrammar 14の問題に解答し、「語彙・文法クイズ」に備える。
② Part 7の英文をチャンク単位で全文和訳をする。

語彙・文法クイズ

Vocabulary 1 ~ 14とGrammar 1 ~ 14から5問(日本語→英語)

Vocabulary 14

Audio② 35

1 ~ 10の語句を英語にしましょう。その後で音声を聞いて確認しましょう。

1. 去年と比べると	______________ to last year
2. 日焼け止めを塗る	___________ on sunscreen
3. 飛行機が遅れている。	The flight is ______________ .
4. 天気が回復した。	The weather has ______________ .
5. 一日中~して過ごす	____________ all day ~ ing
6. 楽しい一日	a ___________ day
7. (携帯で)メールします。	I'll ___________ you.
8. ~するのはどうですか。	___________ about ~ ing?
9. そう言ってはみたものの、…	Having ___________ that, ...
10. 物価が高い。	______________ are high.

Grammar 14

Audio② 36

1 ～ 5の空所を埋めましょう。その後で、音声を聞いて確認しましょう。

1. 私はサッカーの試合を見ることが好きです。

   I like ______________ soccer games.

2. 私は彼が言い訳をするのが好きではありません。

   I don't like _________ making excuses.

3. 彼との話は終わりましたか。

   Have you finished ______________ with him?

4. 私たちはパーティーでおしゃべりを楽しみました。

   We enjoyed ______________ at the party.

5. 私に微笑みながら、彼女は「こんにちは」と言った。

   She said "Hello," ______________ at me.

Pair Practice

・Vocabulary 14を、瞬時に「日本語→英語」にできるように、ペア（AとB）を組んで練習しましょう（1分間）。1分後にAとBの役割を交換し、同様に練習しましょう（1分間）。

A: 教科書を見ながらBに日本語を与える

B: 教科書を閉じたままAが与える日本語を英語にする

A: Bが即答できなければ、すぐにその英語を教え、1分間の内にどの語句もスラスラ英語で言えるようにさせる

・Grammar 14の例文についても同様の練習をしましょう（1分間）。

Grammar Review 14

動名詞と分詞構文

動名詞　：~ing　　　～すること
分詞構文：1）現在分詞〈「～している状態」を伴って〉
　　　　　2）過去分詞〈「～された状態」を伴って〉

【動名詞】 動詞の意味を持ちながら名詞として使われる ~ing のことを動名詞と呼びます。一般に「～すること」のように訳されます。これは不定詞の名詞的用法（～すること）と似ていますが、内包する意味には若干の差があります。空所を埋めながら確認・整理しましょう。

動名詞：~ing（～すること）
Masao likes ____________ comics. （正雄はマンガを読むことが好きです） His parents don't like ____________ **reading** comics. （彼の両親は、正雄の（正雄が）マンガを読むことを好んでいません）

比較：動名詞と不定詞（名詞的用法）

	動名詞（~ing）	不定詞（to ~）
和訳	（実際に）～する（している）こと	（これから）～すること
含み	現実、または実績	非現実、または概念
時間	現在、または過去	未来、または無し

動名詞と不定詞には上のような違いがあるため、以下のようなことが起こります。
○は自然、×は不自然

○ I want **to play** tennis tomorrow.（私は明日テニスをしたい）
× I want playing tennis tomorrow. ← 不自然
○ I remember **meeting** you before.（私はあなたに以前お会いしたことを覚えています）
× I remember to meet you before. ← 不自然
○ I remember **to go out** with you tomorrow.（私は明日あなたと出かけるのを覚えています）
× I remember going out with you tomorrow. ← 不自然

【分詞構文】 分詞構文は下表のように、1) 現在分詞を使うものと、2) 過去分詞を使うものの2種類があります。いずれも例文の空所を埋めながら、確認・整理しましょう。

分詞構文	
1) 現在分詞によるもの	**「～している状態」をともなって** They listened to the lecture, **asking** questions from time to time. （彼らは講義を聞いた　　　　／時折 質問をしながら） **Having rehearsed** a lot, I was not nervous at all.（完了） （十分にリハーサルをしていた状態で／私は全く緊張していなかった）

2) 過去分詞によるもの	「～された状態」をともなって **Compared** to the previous year, we are doing pretty well this year. (前年と比較して(私たちが前年と比較されれば)／私たちは、今年はかなりよくやっている)

▶動名詞：意味上の主語「～の(が)…すること」

① His parents don't like Masao's reading comics.
② His parents don't like his reading comics.
③ His parents don't like Masao reading comics.
④ His parents don't like him reading comics.

reading comicsは「マンガを読むこと」。①はreading comicsの前にMasao'sがあるので「正雄のマンガを読むこと」。この「正雄の」は言い換えれば「正雄が」であり、「～すること」の意味の上での主語（意味上の主語）になっています。このMasao'sは代名詞にすればhis（彼の）になり、②のような文になります。また、口語では③のように、単にMasaoとすることが少なくありません。これは動詞の目的語になっているので、これを代名詞にするとhimになり、④のような文ができます。

▶完了形の動名詞と動名詞の否定：having＋過去分詞(～したこと)

・I'm sorry for **not having answered** sooner.
すみません／もっと早くに返事をしなかったことに対して。

▶動名詞と不定詞

① I like **reading** comics.（私はマンガを読むことが好きです）
② I like **to read** comics.（私はマンガを読むことが好きです）

①と②のように、動詞がlikeだと目的語が動名詞でも不定詞でもあまり意味は変わりません。このような動詞はたくさんあります。注意しなければならないのは、目的語が動名詞と不定詞では意味が異なってくる動詞と、目的語に動名詞しか取らない動詞です。

【目的語が動名詞と不定詞では意味が異なる動詞】remember, forget, tryなど

- remember to ~（～することを覚えている）
- remember ~ing（～したことを覚えている）
- forget to ~（～することを忘れる）
- forget ~ing（～したことを忘れる）
- try to ~（～しようとする）：I tried to eat it.（私はそれを食べようとした）
- try ~ing（実際に～してみる）：I tried eating it.（私はそれを試食した）

【目的語に動名詞しか取らない動詞】stop, finish, give up, enjoy, mind, consider, put offなど
これらの動詞は目的語に不定詞は取らず動名詞のみを取ります。その理由は前の表（p. 113 比較：動名詞と不定詞）で述べている「含み」のためですが、上に記した6つの動詞については理屈抜きに、enjoy playing tennis や finish eating のようにing形と一緒に口で覚えるとよいでしょう。

▶分詞構文

・They listened to the lecture, **asking** questions from time to time.
主役の節　脇役：同時に起こっていること

この文の主役は They listened to the lectureです。asking 以下は、主役に付随する脇役（同時に起こっていること）です。従って「時折質問をしながら、彼らは講義を聞いた」となります。文頭から訳す場合には、「彼らは講義を聞いた、そして時折質問をした」のように andで結び付けるようにして訳してもよいでしょう。

Exercises for the TOEIC® L&R Test

Part 5 Select the best answer to complete each sentence.

1. I remember _______ at this cottage for a week in the summer several years ago.
(A) stay
(B) to stay
(C) stayed
(D) staying

2. Peter is only 15 years old and all his family are against _______ going to India alone.
(A) their
(B) his
(C) them
(D) my

3. _______ last year, more people seem to take longer vacations this year.
(A) As to
(B) Talking about
(C) Compared to
(D) According to

4. Don't _______ to put on sunscreen when you go to the beach as the sun is very strong.
(A) forget
(B) remember
(C) stop
(D) consider

5. At his company everyone can take a three-week vacation _______ having worked for 15 years.
(A) as
(B) because
(C) though
(D) after

Part 6 Select the best answer to complete the text.

TO: Patricia
FROM: Anne
DATE: Oct. 23
RE: Hello from Paris

Hi Pat,
James and I arrived here in Paris two days ago. Our flight was delayed by two hours and it rained **–1–** on the first day. But the weather has improved and we are now enjoying our vacation. We couldn't go out on the first day, **–2–** our hotel is very big and there are many famous shops and restaurants in the hotel. **–3–**. James, as usual, spent all day playing games in the room. Yesterday, we enjoyed **–4–** along the Seine River and then went to the Louvre to enjoy the "city of arts." Today, we're going to the Eiffel Tower. The weather is fine and it will be a fun day. I'll text you again with some photos.

Anne

1. (A) correctly
(B) heavily
(C) smoothly
(D) hopefully

2. (A) because
(B) so
(C) and
(D) but

3. (A) So, I stayed in my room all day watching TV.
(B) So, I went out for shopping downtown with James.
(C) So, I was able to do shopping and have a wonderful lunch here.
(D) So, I went to bed earlier than usual, feeling very tired.

4. (A) to walk
(B) to walking
(C) walking
(D) walked

Part 7 Read the text-message chain and choose the best answer to each question.

Wendy [20:00]: What should we do for our next vacation?

Eric [20:02]: Well, I like traveling, so how about going abroad again? Last year I chose Europe, so this time you can choose.

Wendy [20:03]: I'd like to go somewhere different this year.

Eric [20:04]: How about Oceania?

Wendy [20:06]: Not bad. I went to Australia when I was 5 or 6. I remember hugging a koala there.

Eric [20:08]: Australia is nice, and I'd like to go to New Zealand, too. Having said that, the prices there are quite high compared to those in Europe.

Wendy [20:10]: Don't worry! We won't stay for so long.

1. What are they talking about?
   (A) The history of Europe
   (B) The climate in Oceania
   (C) A zoo in Australia
   (D) A holiday plan

2. At 20:08, what does Eric mean when he writes, "Having said that"?
   (A) Therefore I said that
   (B) Because I said that
   (C) Even though I said that
   (D) That's why I said that

3. What is Eric worried about their next trip?
   (A) Security
   (B) Costs
   (C) Weather
   (D) Food

CHAPTER 15

関係代名詞

Business Performances

本章での学習

▶文法：関係代名詞の復習・確認
▶話題：Business Performances
▶演習：Part 5 → Part 1 → Part 2 → Part 3 → Part 4形式の問題演習

事前学習

① Vocabulary 15とGrammar 15の問題に解答し、「語彙・文法クイズ」に備える。
② Part 3の音声を聞き、ディクテーション（書き取り）をする。

語彙・文法クイズ

Vocabulary 1 〜 15とGrammar 1 〜 15から5問（日本語→英語）

Vocabulary 15

Audio② 37

1 〜 10の語句を英語にしましょう。その後で音声を聞いて確認しましょう。

1.	彼の意見を反映する	reflect his ______________
2.	市場を拡大する	expand a ______________
3.	発展途上国	______________ countries
4.	彼らはみな拍手をしている。	They are all ______________ their hands.
5.	売上を上げる	______________ sales
6.	緊急会議を招集する	______________ an urgent meeting
7.	彼は動揺している。	He is ______________ .
8.	重い空気（雰囲気）	______________ atmosphere
9.	新製品を発売する	launch a new ______________
10.	最悪の状況を乗り切る	overcome the ______________ situation

Grammar 15

Audio② 38

1～5の空所を埋めましょう。その後で、音声を聞いて確認しましょう。

1. 私には、フランス語をとても上手に話す友人がいます。

   I have a friend ________ speaks French very well.

2. 私には、その父親がかつてプロのサッカー選手だった友人がいます。

   I have a friend __________ father used to be a pro soccer player.

3. 1週間前に買ったばかりの自転車が盗まれました。

   The bicycle __________ I bought just a week ago was stolen.

4. 私は彼の言ったことが信じられません。

   I can't believe ________ he said.

5. 彼は病気だと言ったが、それは本当ではなかった。

   He said he was sick, __________ was not true.

Pair Practice

・Vocabulary 15を、瞬時に「日本語→英語」にできるように、ペア(AとB)を組んで練習しましょう(1分間)。1分後にAとBの役割を交換し、同様に練習しましょう(1分間)。

A: 教科書を見ながらBに日本語を与える

B: 教科書を閉じたままAが与える日本語を英語にする

A: Bが即答できなければ、すぐにその英語を教え、1分間の内にどの語句もスラスラ英語で言えるようにさせる

・Grammar 15の例文についても同様の練習をしましょう(1分間)。

Grammar Review 15

関係代名詞

名詞(先行詞)← 関係代名詞 (who, which, that, what) ………

「関係代名詞」とは、「関係づける」「代名詞」、つまり接続詞(接着剤)と代名詞の両方の機能を持ち、名詞を後ろから飾る修飾節を作ります (Grammar Review 2)。関係代名詞にはwho, which, that, whatの4つがあり、先行詞(飾られる名詞)によって使い分けられます。例文の空所を埋めながら確認・整理しましょう。

先行詞と関係代名詞	例 文
1. 「人」: who (thatも可)	the man ________ helped me 「人 ← 私を助けた」 the girl (**whom [who]**) I helped 「少女 ← 私が助けた」 a man **whose** name is Tanaka 「人 ←(その)名前が田中」 ・This is the man ________ helped me. ・This is the girl (**whom [who]**) I helped. (目的格の関係代名詞: 省略可) ・A man **whose** name is Tanaka helped me.
2. 「物」: which / that いずれでも可	a book ____________ moved me 「本 ← 私を感動させた」 the book (**which**) he recommended 「本 ← 彼が薦めた」 the book **whose** cover is red 「本 ←(その)表紙が赤い」 ・This is a book ____________ moved me recently. ・This is the book (**which**) he recommended. (目的格: 省略可) ・The book **whose** cover is red is mine. (whoseはwhichの所有格)
3. 「特別な物・人」: thatが好まれる	先行詞が「特別な物・人」の場合、関係代名詞はthatが好まれる。 「特別な」とは、「唯一」(the only)、「最」(the most, the first)、「全」(all, every, any)、「無」(no)、「同」(the same)などの修飾語を伴うとき。 ・This is the __________ book **that** I read this year. (これが唯一の本です/私が今年読んだ) ・She is the __________ intelligent woman **that** I have ever met. (彼女は最も知的な女性です/私が今まで会ったことのある)
4. 無い: what	what we discussed 「こと/もの ← 私たちが話し合った」 ・This is what we discussed yesterday. (これが、私たちが昨日話し合ったことです)
非制限用法 whichと whoのみ	以上の例は、前の名詞(先行詞)を飾るもので制限用法 以下は非制限用法: 前の名詞・節(先行詞)の情報を追加する用法 ..., which ~ 「…、で、それは(を) ~」 ..., who ~ 「…、で、その人(たち)は(を) ~」

	・I attended a seminar yesterday,__________ was not at all interesting. （私は昨日セミナーに参加した、で、それは全く面白くなかった） ・I met a man at the university,_________ became my husband later. （私は大学で一人の男性に出会いました、で、その人が後に私の夫になりました）

▶関係代名詞が関わるちょっと複雑な文

「これが、私が生まれた家です」を英語にしてみましょう。

・まずは「私が生まれた家」を英語にします。

家 ＋ 私はその家で生まれた
the house ＋ I was born in the house
which
（接着剤：接着部分に移動）

① the house **which** I was born in
家 ／ 私が生まれた → 私が生まれた家

・実はもう１つできます。前置詞とその後の語（前置詞の目的語）は仲良しです。そのため、接着剤whichが接着部分に移動する際、前置詞も一緒に連れていくことがあります。

the house ＋ I was born in the house.
in which
（接着剤）

② the house in **which** I was born → 私が生まれた家

・この①と②の前に This is を言えばできあがり！

This is + ① → This is the house **which** I was born in. ③
This is + ② → This is the house in **which** I was born. ④

③の文は前置詞で終わっていて何か妙な感じがします。また、④は関係代名詞の前に前置詞があり、これも何か複雑に見えます。しかし、上記のように自分で作ってみると納得できますね。

▶関係代名詞の非制限用法

関係代名詞の基本は前の名詞（先行詞）を飾る制限用法ですが、同時に、表の最下段に書かれているように非制限用法もあります。この用法は先行詞（前の名詞・節）の情報を追加することから追叙用法とも呼ばれています。「… and 代名詞」のように理解するとよいでしょう。

・I attended a seminar yesterday, **which** was not at all interesting.
(and it)
私は昨日セミナーに参加した、で、それは全く面白くなかった。

・I met a man at the university, **who** became my husband later.
(and he)
私は大学で一人の男性に出会いました、で、その人が後に私の夫になりました。

・She spent five years in London because of her father's job, **which** I didn't know until recently.
(and it)
彼女は父親の仕事の都合で、5年間ロンドンで過ごしました、で、そのことを私は最近まで知りませんでした。

この用法は文章だけでなく、会話でもよく使われます。読むときには「,」（カンマ）を見落とさないように。聞くときには文脈で制限用法か非制限用法かを判断しましょう。

Exercises for the TOEIC® L&R Test

Part 5 Select the best answer to complete each sentence.

1. The air conditioner ________ you can control with your smartphone is not selling very well.
(A) what
(B) which
(C) who
(D) in which

2. Mr. Jones is an excellent sales person ________ sells more than 50 houses every year.
(A) which
(B) whose
(C) what
(D) who

3. This is the new project team _______ Ms. Jasmin Anderson is working as the leader.
(A) that
(B) on which
(C) what
(D) who

4. When we set sales targets, we need to reflect ______ the manager expects.
(A) which
(B) who
(C) whose
(D) what

5. We should expand our market to developing countries _______ population is over 50 million.
(A) whose
(B) that
(C) what
(D) which

Part 1 Listen and select the one statement that best describes what you see in the picture. Audio② 39-41

1.

Ⓐ Ⓑ Ⓒ Ⓓ

2.

Ⓐ Ⓑ Ⓒ Ⓓ

Part 2 Listen and select the best response to each question or statement. Audio② 42-46

1. Ⓐ Ⓑ Ⓒ　2. Ⓐ Ⓑ Ⓒ　3. Ⓐ Ⓑ Ⓒ　4. Ⓐ Ⓑ Ⓒ

Part 3 Listen and select the best answer to each question. Audio② 47-49

1. What kind of meeting are they talking about?
   (A) A kickoff meeting
   (B) A monthly meeting
   (C) A planning meeting
   (D) A sales meeting

2. Who is Mr. Baker?
   (A) A new manager
   (B) A new employee
   (C) A new client
   (D) A new president

3. What does the man mean when he says, "So, he was very upset"?
   (A) He was very happy.
   (B) He was very angry.
   (C) He was very tired.
   (D) He was very satisfied.

Part 4 Listen and select the best answer to each question. **Audio② 50-52**

1. Who are the listeners?
   (A) Clients
   (B) New staff
   (C) Employees
   (D) Temporary staff

2. What is the speaker worried about?
   (A) Employment
   (B) A customer complaint
   (C) Sales
   (D) Office atmosphere

3. What does the speaker ask the listeners to do?
   (A) Give opinions
   (B) Go on a business trip
   (C) Hand out documents
   (D) Develop a new product

CHAPTER 16

関係副詞

Handling Customer Complaints

本章での学習

▶文法：関係副詞の復習・確認
▶話題：Handling Customer Complaints
▶演習：Part 5 → Part 6 → Part 7形式の問題演習

事前学習

① Vocabulary 16とGrammar 16の問題に解答し、「語彙・文法クイズ」に備える。
② Part 7の英文をチャンク単位で全文和訳をする。

語彙・文法クイズ

Vocabulary 1 ～ 16とGrammar 1 ～ 16から5問(日本語→英語)

Vocabulary 16

Audio② 53

1～10の語句を英語にしましょう。その後で音声を聞いて確認しましょう。

1. 品物を購入する　purchase an ____________
2. 苦情に対処する　____________ with complaints
3. よくある間違い　________________ mistake
4. 新たな仕事の機会につながる　____________ to new business opportunities
5. 問題を解決する　solve the ________________
6. ご意見ありがとうございます。　Thank you for your ______________ .
7. 詳しく説明する　________________ it in detail
8. あなたに迷惑をかける　cause you ________________
9. 遅くとも　at the ________________
10. 送料　__________________ cost

Grammar 16

Audio② 54

1～5の空所を埋めましょう。その後で、音声を聞いて確認しましょう。

1. ここが、私が生まれた家です。
   This is the house ___________ I was born.

2. だれか彼が欠席している理由を知っていますか。
   Does anyone know the reason _________ he is absent?

3. 最終バスが出る時間をご存知ですか。
   Do you know the time _________ the last bus leaves?

4. 駅への行き方を教えて頂けますか。
   Could you tell me _________ I can get to the station?

5. 私は京都に行き、そこで観光を楽しみました。
   I went to Kyoto, ___________ I enjoyed sightseeing.

Pair Practice

・Vocabulary 16を、瞬時に「日本語→英語」にできるように、ペア(AとB)を組んで練習しましょう(1分間)。1分後にAとBの役割を交換し、同様に練習しましょう(1分間)。

A: 教科書を見ながらBに日本語を与える

B: 教科書を閉じたままAが与える日本語を英語にする

A: Bが即答できなければ、すぐにその英語を教え、1分間の内にどの語句もスラスラ英語で言えるようにさせる

・Grammar 16の例文についても同様の練習をしましょう(1分間)。

Grammar Review 16

関係副詞

名詞(先行詞)← 関係副詞(when, where, how, why)…

「関係副詞」とは、「関係づける」「副詞」、つまり接続詞(接着剤)と副詞の両方の機能を持ち、場所や時などを表す名詞(先行詞)を後ろから飾る修飾節を作ります(Grammar Review 2)。関係副詞にはwhen, where, how, whyの4つがあり、先行詞によって使い分けられます。例文の空所を埋めながら確認・整理しましょう。

先行詞 関係副詞	例　文
1) 場所: where	the room **where** we have the meeting　部屋 ← 私たちがその会議をする ・This is the room ＿＿＿＿＿ we have the meeting. (ここが、私たちがその会議をする部屋です)
2) 時: when	the day **when** we first met.　日 ← 私達が初めて会った ・Do you remember the day ＿＿＿＿＿ we first met? (私たちが初めて会った日を覚えていますか)
3) 方法・様態: how	the way **how** he speaks　方法 ← 彼が話す ・I don't like the way he speaks.　← howの省略 ・I don't like ＿＿＿＿＿ he speaks.　← the wayの省略 (私は彼のしゃべり方が好きではない) 注意:the wayまたはhowのいずれかを必ず省略 × I don't like the way how he speaks.
4) 理由: why	the reason **why** he is absent　理由 ← 彼が休んでいる ・Do you know (the reason) **why** he is absent? ・Do you know the reason (why) he is absent? (あなたは彼が休んでいる理由を知っていますか) 注意:the reasonかwhyのいずれかの省略可
非制限用法 whereと whenのみ	以上の例は、前の名詞(先行詞)を飾るもので制限用法 以下は非制限用法:前の名詞(先行詞)の情報を追加する ..., where ~　「…、で、そこで(に) ~」 ..., when ~　「…、で、そのとき~」 ・I went to Australia, ＿＿＿＿＿ I enjoyed sightseeing. (私はオーストラリアに行きました、で、そこで観光を楽しみました) ・We'll have a meeting on Friday, ＿＿＿＿＿ the schedule will be announced. (金曜日に会議をします、で、そのとき、スケジュールが発表されます)

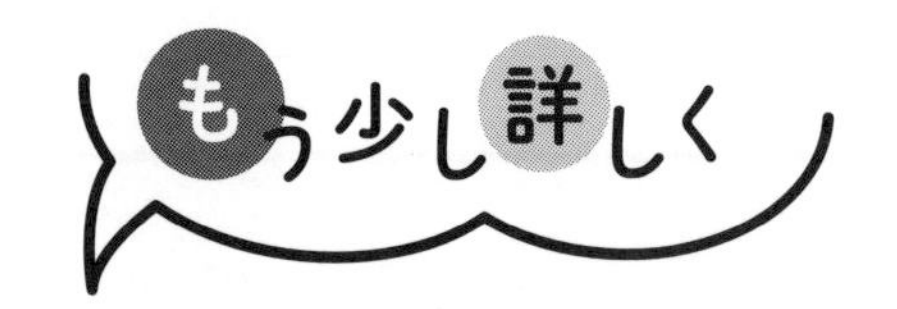

▶関係副詞・先行詞の省略

the way how とthe reason why の省略については表に示している通りです。省略の理由は、how自体に先行詞wayと同じ意味が含まれていて、同様に、why自体に先行詞reasonと同じ意味が含まれているためです。こうした省略はwhereとwhenについても先行詞によっては起こります。

where **先行詞がthe placeの場合 — whereかthe placeのいずれかの省略可**

① This is the place **where** we first met. ⬅ 省略無し
② This is the place we first met. ⬅ whereの省略
③ This is **where** we first met. ⬅ the placeの省略
(ここは私たちが初めて出会った場所です)

when

・先行詞がthe timeの場合 — whenかthe timeのいずれかの省略可

① Now is the time **when** we should start. ⬅ 省略無し
② Now is the time we should start. ⬅ whenの省略
③ Now is **when** we should start. ⬅ the timeの省略
(今が出発すべき時です)

・先行詞がthe dayの場合 — whenの省略可

① Do you remember the day **when** we first met? ⬅ 省略無し
② Do you remember the day we first met? ⬅ whenの省略
(私たちが初めて会った日を覚えていますか)

▶関係副詞の非制限用法

関係代名詞と同様に、関係副詞にも先行詞（前の名詞）について情報を追加する非制限用法（追叙用法）があります。「… and 副詞」のように理解するとよいでしょう。

・I went to Australia, **where** I enjoyed sightseeing.
(and there)
私はオーストラリアに行きました、で、そこで観光を楽しみました。

・We'll meet on Friday, **when** the schedule will be announced.
(and then)
私たちは金曜日に会合します、で、そのときスケジュールが発表されます。

関係副詞の非制限用法はwhereとwhenの場合だけです。文章だけでなく、会話でもよく使われます。読むときには「,」（カンマ）を見落とさないように。聞くときには文脈で制限用法か非制限用法かを判断しましょう。

Exercises for the TOEIC® L&R Test

Part 5 Select the best answer to complete each sentence.

1. The woman is angry about ______ they serve customers at the restaurant.
(A) while
(B) where
(C) why
(D) the way

2. First of all, we should find out ______ the customer is not happy about our services.
(A) the time
(B) the reason
(C) the way
(D) the place

3. Check the receipt that says the date and time ______ the customer purchased the item.
(A) where
(B) why
(C) when
(D) how

4. There is a room ______ you can have free drinks and refreshments while waiting.
(A) where
(B) how
(C) why
(D) when

5. I worked at a hotel for three years, ______ I learned how to deal with customer complaints.
(A) which
(B) how
(C) that
(D) when

Part 6 Select the best answer to complete the text.

HOW TO HANDLE CUSTOMER COMPLAINTS

Customer complaints are common in business, but it is not a happy experience. **–1–**, if you **–2–** them well, it can lead to new business opportunities. **–3–**. First, remember the following four basic steps.

STEP 1. Understand the customer's feelings.
STEP 2. Try to find out the reason **–4–** it happened.
STEP 3. Present a plan to solve the problem.
STEP 4. Apologize and thank them for their input.

Look at each of these four steps in detail in the next section.

1. (A) Therefore
(B) Unfortunately
(C) Moreover
(D) However

2. (A) handle
(B) handled
(C) to handle
(D) handling

3. (A) Some people get angry and shout loudly.
(B) All of the questions should be short and clear.
(C) Then, how do you successfully take care of complaints?
(D) This is how we solved the problem.

4. (A) when
(B) where
(C) what
(D) why

Part 7 Read the e-mails and choose the best answer to each question.

To: Henry Nelson
From: Susie Ikeda
Date: November 17
Subject: Wrong delivery

Dear Mr. Nelson,

The items we ordered on November 10 arrived this morning. However, although we ordered three office desks, we received three chairs instead. We have to rearrange our office for new employees who will join us at the end of November. Please let me know as soon as possible when you can send us the desks. Also, tell me what to do with the chairs you sent us in error.

Sincerely yours,

Susie Ikeda

To: Susie Ikeda
From: Henry Nelson
Date: November 17
Subject: Re: Wrong delivery

Dear Ms. Ikeda,

Please accept our deepest apologies for causing you trouble with the wrong shipment. We will send the correct items immediately. You will receive them in two days at the latest.

This type of error is very unusual. Now we are trying to find out why and how this has happened. We promise that such errors will not happen again.

As for the chairs we shipped, could you please send them back to us? We are very sorry for the trouble. Of course, we will cover the shipping cost.

Again, we apologize for the inconvenience this has caused.

Yours sincerely,

Henry Nelson
Manager, Shipping Department

1. What is the purpose of the first e-mail?
(A) To apologize
(B) To complain
(C) To place an order
(D) To make an appointment

2. What does Ms. Ikeda have to do by the end of November?
(A) Change the office arrangement
(B) Hire new staff
(C) Move the office
(D) Place another order

3. What will Ms. Ikeda most likely do with the chairs?
(A) Keep them in her office
(B) Throw them away
(C) Send them back
(D) Sell them to a recycling shop

4. When will Ms. Ikeda probably receive the desks?
(A) November 10
(B) November 17
(C) November 19
(D) November 22

5. In the second e-mail, the word "cover" in paragraph 3, line 2 is closest in meaning to
(A) pay
(B) cut
(C) reduce
(D) increase

CHAPTER 17

比較

Environment

本章での学習

▶文法：比較の復習・確認
▶話題：Environment
▶演習：Part 5 → Part 1 → Part 2 → Part 3 → Part 4形式の問題演習

事前学習

① Vocabulary 17とGrammar 17の問題に解答し、「語彙・文法クイズ」に備える。
② Part 3の音声を聞き、ディクテーション(書き取り)をする。

語彙・文法クイズ

Vocabulary 1 ～ 17とGrammar 1 ～ 17から5問(日本語→英語)

Vocabulary 17

Audio② 55

1 ～ 10の語句を英語にしましょう。その後で音声を聞いて確認しましょう。

1. 深刻な社会問題　＿＿＿＿＿＿＿＿ social problem
2. 環境保護　environmental ＿＿＿＿＿＿＿＿
3. 汚染された河川　＿＿＿＿＿＿＿＿ river
4. 絶滅危惧の動物　＿＿＿＿＿＿＿＿＿＿ animals
5. 電気自動車の利点　advantage of ＿＿＿＿＿＿＿＿ cars
6. それは面倒だ。　It's ＿＿＿＿＿＿＿＿＿＿＿ .
7. エレベーターの代わりに階段を使う　use stairs ＿＿＿＿＿＿＿＿ of an elevator
8. エネルギー効率のよいのと交換する　＿＿＿＿＿＿ it with an energy-efficient one
9. 長い目で見ると　in the long ＿＿＿＿＿＿
10. 冷蔵庫　＿＿＿＿＿＿＿＿＿＿＿

Grammar 17

Audio② 56

1～5の空所を埋めましょう。その後で、音声を聞いて確認しましょう。

1. 弟は私よりも背が高い。

   My younger brother is ____________ than I.

2. 彼女はクラスの女子の中で食べるのが一番速い。

   She eats the ____________ of all the girls in her class.

3. あなたにとって命よりも大事なものは何ですか。

   What is _________ important to you than life?

4. 中国語は英語ほど難しくない。

   Chinese is not as difficult _________ English.

5. 東京タワーは日本で2番目に高いタワーです。

   Tokyo Tower is the ____________ highest tower in Japan.

Pair Practice

・Vocabulary 17を、瞬時に「日本語→英語」にできるように、ペア（AとB）を組んで練習しましょう（1分間）。1分後にAとBの役割を交換し、同様に練習しましょう（1分間）。

A: 教科書を見ながらBに日本語を与える

B: 教科書を閉じたままAが与える日本語を英語にする

A: Bが即答できなければ、すぐにその英語を教え、1分間の内にどの語句もスラスラ英語で言えるようにさせる

・Grammar 17の例文についても同様の練習をしましょう（1分間）。

Grammar Review 17

比較

1. 原形 ：A … as ～ as B. (Aは同じくらい～／Bと比べ)
2. 比較級：A … ～er / more ～ than B. (Aはより～／Bよりも)
3. 最上級：A … the ～est / most ～ in B / of C (Aは最も～／Bの中で／Cの内で)

「比較」の表現には3パターンあります。1. 形容詞、副詞をそのままの形（原級）で使うもの、2. 形容詞、副詞に –er、または more ... を加えた形（比較級）を使うもの、3. 形容詞、副詞に –est、または most ... を加えた形（最上級）を使うものです。more, mostは形容詞、副詞が長い語（2音節以上、ただし2音節でも〈子音字+y〉、-er、-leで終わる語は除く）に対して -erや -estの代わりに使います。例文の空所を埋めながら確認・整理しましょう。

形容詞・副詞	例　文
1. 原級（同等） (～)	1) 基本：A ... as ~ as B.（Aは同じくらい～／Bと比べて） Tom works **as** hard **as** Mary. （トムは同じくらい熱心に働く／メアリーと比べ） 2) 否定：A ... not ... as ~ as B（Aは～ではない／Bと比べて） Tom does ＿＿＿＿ work **as** hard **as** Mary. （トムは（同じくらい）熱心には働かない／メアリーと比べ（ほど））
2. 比較級 (~er) (more ~) (less ~)	1) 基本：A ... ~er than B.（Aはより～／Bよりも） Mary works hard**er** ＿＿＿＿ Tom. （メアリーはより熱心に働く／トムよりも） 2) 基本：A ... more ~ than B.（Aはより～／Bよりも） Your smartphone is ＿＿＿＿ expensive than mine. （あなたのスマホはより値段が高い／私のよりも） 3) less（より少なく～＝比較的～でない）を使った表現 My smartphone is ＿＿＿＿ expensive than yours. （私のスマホは高くない／あなたのより） 4) 繰り返しを避けるthat：that of ~（～のそれ） The population of Japan is larger than **that** of Australia. （日本の人口は多い／オーストラリアのそれよりも）

3. 最上級 (the ~est)	1) 基本：A ... the ~est in B（Aは最も～／Bの中で） He is __________ busi**est** in his section. （彼は最も忙しい／彼の部署の中で）
(the most ~)	2) 基本：A ... the most ~ in B（Aは最も～／Bの中で） She is **the** __________ efficient in her section. （彼女は最も仕事ができる／彼女の部署の中で）
副詞の場合は theの省略可	3) 基本：A ... the ~est of C（Aは最も～／Cの内で） He is **the** busiest **of** the five members. （彼が最も忙しい／5人の内で） 注意：in ~ と of ~ の違い（Grammar Review 10参照）
	inは「範囲」—「～という場所の中で」 ofは「分離」—「～（同類）の内から」 ofの場合はたいてい後ろにallや数が来る。
(the least ~)	4) least（最も少なく～＝最も～でない）を使った表現 He is **the** __________ busy in his section. （彼は最も忙しくない／彼の部署の中で）

▶比較を含んだ慣用表現

比較は多くの慣用表現の中で使われています。一見複雑そうですが、基本をしっかりつかんでおくと、容易に理解できます。

1. 原級を用いたもの

・「～倍」：A ... X times as ~ as B（AはX倍～／Bと比べて）
Mary works **three times as** hard **as** Tom.（メアリーは3倍熱心に働く／トムと比べ）
「同等」の表現で「メアリーの側」に掛け算をしたもの。2倍はtwice、3倍以上は「基数詞＋times」。

2. 比較級を用いたもの

① The 比較級…, the 比較級～（…であればあるほど、その分、より～）
The sooner you do it, **the better** it is.（早くやればやるほど、その分、よりよい）
2つの比較級を強調するためにthe soonerとthe betterが文頭に移動しています。このtheは「その分～」（副詞）を表します。

② no more than ~（～しか）

I made **no more than** two errors in the exam.（私は試験で2問しか間違えなかった）

noは強い否定。more than two errors（2つより多い間違い）を強く否定すると「数で2つを超えない」「多いどころか少ない」となり、「～しか（そんなに少ない）」という意味に。

③ no less than ~（～も）

He made **no less than** 15 errors in the exam.（彼は試験で15問も間違えた）

これは②の反対。less than 15 errors（15より少ない）を強く否定すると、「数で15を下らない」「少ないどころか多い」となり、「～も（そんなに多い）」という意味に。

④ A ... no more ~ than B（Aは全く～でない／ B同様に）

This philosophy book is **no more** difficult **than** a comic book.

（この哲学書は全く難しくない／マンガ本同様に）

more difficult than a comic book（マンガ本より難しい）をnoで強く否定すると「難しさでマンガ本を上回ることはない」「難しいどころではない（簡単だ）」となり、「マンガ本同様に全く難しくない」となります。

3. 最上級を用いたもの

① the 序数詞 ~est / most ~（X番目に最も～な）

He is **the second** busi**est** man in his section.

busiestの前にsecondがあるので「2番目に最も忙しい」。「3番目」ならthird、「4番目」ならfourthのように序数詞を使います。

② one of the ~est / most ~（最も～のひとり／ひとつ）

He is **one of the** busi**est** employee**s** in his section.

one of ~sは「～のひとり／ひとつ」。この文では～にthe busiest employees（最も忙しい社員たち）が言われています。one of ~s の複数のsに注意。

▶比較で「程度」を表す副詞： much, a lot, a little, by ~など

1. 「ずっと～」： much / a lot / far

Mary works **much** harder than Tom.（メアリーはずっと熱心に働く／トムよりも）

2. 「少しだけ～」：a little

Tom is **a little** taller than Mary.（トムは少しだけ背が高い／メアリーよりも）

3. 「～の差で」： 差異を表す by ~

Tom is taller than Mary **by** 3cm.（トムは背が高い／メアリーより／ 3センチ差で）

Exercises for the TOEIC® L&R Test

Part 5 Select the best answer to complete each sentence.

1. Garbage disposal is _______ of the most serious social problems that we face today.
(A) more
(B) one
(C) first
(D) second

2. The city will spend twice ________ much money on environmental protection this year as it did last year.
(A) times
(B) as
(C) more
(D) than

3. _________ people have become interested in their environment due to SDG campaigns.
(A) As
(B) Much
(C) Every
(D) More

4. The average temperature in July this year is higher than last year _______ 0.7 degrees Celsius.
(A) from
(B) of
(C) by
(D) in

5. Many rivers in Brazil are _________ polluted than 20 years ago due to the government's efforts.
(A) as
(B) less
(C) most
(D) much

Part 1 Listen and select the one statement that best describes what you see in the picture. Audio② 57-59

1.

Ⓐ Ⓑ Ⓒ Ⓓ

2.

Ⓐ Ⓑ Ⓒ Ⓓ

Part 2 Listen and select the best response to each question or statement. Audio② 60-64

1. Ⓐ Ⓑ Ⓒ 2. Ⓐ Ⓑ Ⓒ 3. Ⓐ Ⓑ Ⓒ 4. Ⓐ Ⓑ Ⓒ

Part 3 Listen and select the best answer to each question. Audio② 65-67

1. Where did Maggie get the bag?
   (A) An office
   (B) A printing shop
   (C) A volunteer office
   (D) A department store

2. What does Maggie think about carrying her own shopping bag?
   (A) Not convenient
   (B) Not easy
   (C) Not troublesome
   (D) Not good

3. What does Ted's company do to protect the environment?
   (A) Turn off office lights
   (B) Use stairs instead of an elevator
   (C) Print out less documents
   (D) Reuse paper

Part 4 Listen and select the best answer to each question. 

1. How does the speaker feel about environmental protection?
   (A) It's not so difficult.
   (B) It's very difficult.
   (C) It's not so important.
   (D) It's very cheap.

2. What is good about new electrical appliances?
   (A) They are more expensive.
   (B) They are less expensive.
   (C) They need more energy.
   (D) They need less energy.

3. What does the speaker mean when he says, "in the long run"?
   (A) before long
   (B) at first
   (C) in the end
   (D) in the beginning

CHAPTER 18

名詞と冠詞

Housing

本章での学習

▶文法：名詞と冠詞の復習・確認
▶話題：Housing
▶演習：Part 5 → Part 6 → Part 7形式の問題演習

事前学習

① Vocabulary 18とGrammar 18の問題に解答し、「語彙・文法クイズ」に備える。
② Part 7の英文（1つ目）をチャンク単位で全文和訳をする。

語彙・文法クイズ

Vocabulary 1 ～ 18とGrammar 1 ～ 18から5問（日本語→英語）

Vocabulary 18

Audio② 71

1 ～ 10の語句を英語にしましょう。その後で音声を聞いて確認しましょう。

1. マンションの間取り	floor ____________ of a condominium
2. 不動産業者	real estate ______________
3. ～に位置している	be ________________ in ～
4. 駅から歩いて7分	a seven-minute ____________ from the station
5. 周囲の風景	surrounding __________________
6. 寝室が2部屋ついています。	It ______________ with two bedrooms.
7. 住宅展示会の会場	venue for a _________________ exhibition
8. 私の転勤のため	____________ to my relocation
9. …を確信しています	We are __________________ that ...
10. バスは20分ごとに出ます。	The bus leaves ______________ 20 minutes.

Grammar 18

Audio② 72

1 ~ 5の空所を埋めましょう。その後で、音声を聞いて確認しましょう。

1. あなたは1週間に何日アルバイトをしていますか。
   How many ________ a week do you work part time?

2. オムレツを作るにはミルク、バター、卵が必要です。
   We need ________ , butter and eggs to make an omelet.

3. 私は月旅行をしたいです。
   I want to travel to ____________ .

4. 飲み物は自動販売機で買えます。
   You can buy ___________ from the vending machine.

5. このカレーには鶏肉が入っていますか。
   Is there any ___________ in this curry?

Pair Practice

・Vocabulary 18を、瞬時に「日本語→英語」にできるように、ペア(AとB)を組んで練習しましょう(1分間)。1分後にAとBの役割を交換し、同様に練習しましょう(1分間)。

A: 教科書を見ながらBに日本語を与える

B: 教科書を閉じたままAが与える日本語を英語にする

A: Bが即答できなければ、すぐにその英語を教え、1分間の内にどの語句もスラスラ英語で言えるようにさせる

・Grammar 18の例文についても同様の練習をしましょう(1分間)。

Grammar Review 18

名詞と冠詞

名詞：可算名詞（数えられる）、不可算名詞（数えられない）
冠詞：定冠詞（the：特定）、不定冠詞（a/an：不特定、可算）、無冠詞（不特定、不可算）

英語は1つの名詞について、日本語より「多め」の情報を提供します。例えば、日本語では「友人と映画に行った」と言います。一緒に行った友人は「1人なのか複数なのか」が分かりません。英語で「友人と」の表現は、with a friend、with friends、with the friend、with the friends のいずれかです。1人なのか複数なのかに加えて、「特定」の友人なのか「不特定」なのかについても常に表わします。空所を埋めながら、まずは基本的なルールを確認・整理しましょう。

名詞：可算名詞と不可算名詞		
	判断の基準	例文
1. 可算名詞 a/an、または複数のsをつける	1) 具体的な形（輪郭、区切り、まとまり）を持つもの 2)「気持ちの中で」具体的な形（輪郭、区切り、まとまった内容）を持つもの	I eat **an apple** a day for my health. （健康のためリンゴを1日1個食べます） I have ______ **good idea**. （いい考えがあります） Three ______ and **two teas**, please. （コーヒー 3つに紅茶2つお願いします）
2. 不可算名詞 a/anや複数のsはつけない	1) 具体的な形を持たないもの 2) 具体的な形がくずれたもの	I want some **water**, please. （水がいくらかほしい） My mother puts some ______ in her curry. （母はカレーにリンゴを入れます）

冠　詞：定冠詞(the：特定)、不定冠詞(a/an：不特定、可算)、無冠詞(不特定、不可算)		
冠　詞	選択の判断基準	例文
1. 特定 theをつける	1) 前の内容をから特定できる(その〜)	I went to China. ______ **trip** was fun. (中国に行きました。その旅は楽しかった)
	2) 状況から特定できる(その〜)	Pass me **the salt**, please. (その塩を取っていただけますか)
	3)「ひとつ(1人)」に特定される	He is ______ **president** of our university. (彼が私たちの大学の学長です)
	4) 全体の中での一部(その総称)を特定する	**The computer** is very helpful. (コンピュータというものはとても便利だ)
2. 不特定 a/an, または無冠詞	特定できないもの	He is ______ **professor** of our university. (彼は私の大学の教授です) I like **coffee** better than **tea**. (私は紅茶よりコーヒーの方が好きです)

▶名詞：こんな名詞が数えられる？

表で気になるのが、名詞1の2) で、「『気持ちの中で』具体的な形（輪郭、区切り、まとまった内容）を持つもの」の部分です。実際に具体的な形を持たないものが、どういう「気持ち」で「具体的な形」につながり可算名詞になっているのか。イメージの中での「輪郭、区切り、まとまった内容」をキーワードに、表中の2つの例文で見ていきましょう。

・I have **a good idea**.
idea（考え）という抽象的なものをなぜ英語では数えられる名詞としているのでしょう。これは気持ちの中で、ひとつの「まとまった内容」というイメージでとらえているのです。thought（考え）、reason（理由）、concept（概念）、story（物語）、dream（夢）などもこの仲間です。

・**Three coffees** and **two teas**, please.
coffeeもteaも液体ですが、カフェで注文するときには商品として、ひとつ、ふたつといったイメージになり、数えられる名詞(可算名詞)に変身します。

・ついでにもうひとつ：There are seven **days** in **a week**.
dayやweekは「時間」であって、目に見える具体的な形はありません。しかし、気持ちの中で時間的な「区切り」をイメージし、「形」にして数えています。break（休憩）やtrip（旅行）なども同様のイメージです。

実際には、「なぜこれが可算名詞／不可算名詞？」と首をひねりたくなるものもあります。例えばadvice（アドバイス）。上記のイメージに当てはめれば、ひとつの「まとまった内容」なのでideaなどと同様に可算名詞ではないだろうかと思いがちです。しかし、実際には不可算名詞です。例外が少なからずあることを前提に、少しずつ慣れるしかありません。

▶定冠詞the：どんなふうに特定？

定冠詞theの最も基本的な意味は「その」で、表の1. 特定 の1) The trip was fun. がこれです。また、2) Pass me the salt, please.も 1) に準じるものです。これらは、「(他のどれでもなく) その旅、その塩」を意味し、「特定性」を持ちます。3)と4)についても見ていきましょう。

・表の1. 特定の3)：「ひとつ(1人)」について
He is **the president** of our university.
これは、1)、2) とは違って、常識的に「ひとり（ひとつ）」と判断されることから、「特定性」を意味するtheが付けられたものです。「私たちの大学の学長」は1人しかいないためです（表の2不特定：He is **a professor** of our university. と比較）。the earth（地球）、the sun（太陽）、the worldなども同じです。

・表の2. 特定の4)：「全体の中での一部(その総称)」について
The computer is very useful.
1)、2)、3) に該当しないのに the computerのように言うことがあります。これは「いろいろな道具(道具という全体)」の中での特定の「コンピュータ(という一部の道具)」という意味であり、コンピュータの「総称」を意味します（「総称」には無冠詞の複数形もよく使われる：Computers are very helpful.）。また、「全体の中での一部」には、in the morningやin the afternoonのtheもその一例です。「1日という全体の中での一部」を意味しています。

名詞の可算か不可算かの判断と同様に、冠詞についてもその選択の判断は一筋縄では行きません。たくさんの英文に触れながら、少しずつ慣れていきましょう。

Exercises for the TOEIC® L&R Test

Part 5 Select the best answer to complete each sentence.

1. I am living in an apartment now, but I want to buy ______ in the near future.
(A) house
(B) a house
(C) housing
(D) houses

2. I liked the floor plan of the condominium, but ______ was too high.
(A) price
(B) a price
(C) prices
(D) the price

3. The real estate agent gave me a lot of ______ about how to choose a good old house.
(A) advices
(B) an advice
(C) advice
(D) the advices

4. Do we have enough ______ ? We are inviting 12 people for the housewarming party, right?
(A) food
(B) foods
(C) a food
(D) the food

5. Our house is located in the center of the city and ______ from the station.
(A) seven-minute walk
(B) seven-minute walks
(C) a seven-minute walk
(D) the seven-minute walk

Part 6 Select the best answer to complete the text.

This cottage is **–1–** 5 miles south of the city of Lewes in England. The peaceful color matches the surrounding landscape and it creates a relaxing atmosphere. It is perfect for those **–2–** want to relax in the comforts of home. It comes **–3–** a kitchen, a living room, two bedrooms and a bathroom. **–4–**. There is a plenty of room for storage, too. The cottage gives you everything you need for your perfect holidays.

1. (A) locate
(B) locating
(C) located
(D) location

2. (A) who
(B) what
(C) which
(D) that

3. (A) of
(B) with
(C) for
(D) from

4. (A) It is only a 30-minute train ride to Gatwick airport.
(B) We are located on the beach with wonderful coastal views.
(C) The nearby market town has many excellent shops and restaurants.
(D) The master bedroom has a walk-in closet and a shower room.

Part 7 Read the e-mails and choose the best answer to each question.

To: Wilson Real Estate
From: Ken Rogers
Date: December 9
Re: Housing exhibition

Dear Sales Manager,

I am looking for a new house due to my relocation. A friend introduced me to your housing exhibition. I would very much like to take the tour next weekend. Could you please give me the details about it? I plan to go by train. Please let me know the nearest station and how to get to the exhibition site from there.

Best regards,
Ken Rogers

To: Ken Rogers
From: Mark Wilson
Date: December 9
Re: Re: Housing exhibition

Dear Mr. Rogers,

Thank you very much for your interest in our housing exhibition. We have been in the real estate business for half a century. Our housing exhibitions have helped many people choose their houses. We are confident that we can recommend a house that will satisfy you.

The schedule for the model house viewing is as follows.
Exhibition days: Every day except Wednesday
Time: 9:00 A.M.-5:00 P.M.
Venue: Our Kingstone exhibition site

To make a reservation, please click on the link below.
https://house.us/j/112112112
We have many visitors on weekends. If you wish to come on a weekend, please make your reservation as early as possible.

If you are coming by train, our shuttle bus leaves Kingstone Station to the venue every 20 minutes. After viewing the model houses, our consultants will be happy to give you some advice.

We are looking forward to seeing you.

Mark Wilson
Sales Manager, Wilson Real Estate

1. What is the purpose of the first e-mail?
(A) To ask about a train service
(B) To ask about an event
(C) To cancel a housing loan
(D) To cancel an appointment

2. When did Wilson Real Estate start business?
(A) 20 years ago
(B) 30 years ago
(C) 40 years ago
(D) 50 years ago

3. How will Mr. Rogers get to the exhibition site from the station?
(A) By car
(B) By taxi
(C) By shuttle bus
(D) By train

4. How can Mr. Rogers apply for this event?
(A) Online
(B) By telephone
(C) By e-mail
(D) By letter

5. How many shuttle buses run in one hour?
(A) One
(B) Two
(C) Three
(D) Four

CHAPTER 19

数と量

Advertising

本章での学習

▶文法：数と量の復習・確認
▶話題：Advertising
▶演習：Part 5 → Part 1 → Part 2 → Part 3 → Part 4形式の問題演習

事前学習

① Vocabulary 19とGrammar 19の問題に解答し、「語彙・文法クイズ」に備える。
② Part 3の音声を聞き、ディクテーション（書き取り）をする。

語彙・文法クイズ

Vocabulary 1 ～ 19とGrammar 1 ～ 19から5問（日本語→英語）

Vocabulary 19

Audio② 73

1 ～ 10の語句を英語にしましょう。その後で音声を聞いて確認しましょう。

1. 広告に投資する ＿＿＿＿＿＿＿＿ in advertisements (ads)
2. 客の注意を引き付ける attract consumers' ＿＿＿＿＿＿＿＿
3. 彼に助言を求める ＿＿＿＿＿＿ him for advice
4. インターネットの普及 ＿＿＿＿＿＿＿＿ of the Internet
5. 20代の女性をターゲットにする ＿＿＿＿＿＿＿＿ women in their 20's
6. 予算を考慮する consider a ＿＿＿＿＿＿＿＿
7. 家電製品店 ＿＿＿＿＿＿＿＿＿ store
8. 10周年を祝う celebrate a 10th ＿＿＿＿＿＿＿＿＿＿
9. 30%の割引を提供する offer a 30% ＿＿＿＿＿＿＿＿
10. 今月末まで続く ＿＿＿＿＿＿ until the end of this month

Grammar 19

Audio② 74

1～5の空所を埋めましょう。その後で、音声を聞いて確認しましょう。

1. 彼女には友人が多い。

   She has a _________ of friends.

2. それに関して2、3質問があります。

   I have a _________ questions about it.

3. 私の妹は新しいジーンズを買いました。

   My sister bought a new _________ of jeans.

4. いくらかワインはいかがですか。

   Would you like _________ wine?

5. 私の水筒にはほとんど水が残っていません。

   There is ____________ water left in my bottle.

Pair Practice

・Vocabulary 19を、瞬時に「日本語→英語」にできるように、ペア（AとB）を組んで練習しましょう（1分間）。1分後にAとBの役割を交換し、同様に練習しましょう（1分間）。

A: 教科書を見ながらBに日本語を与える

B: 教科書を閉じたままAが与える日本語を英語にする

A: Bが即答できなければ、すぐにその英語を教え、1分間の内にどの語句もスラスラ英語で言えるようにさせる

・Grammar 19の例文についても同様の練習をしましょう（1分間）。

Grammar Review 19

数と量

1. 数量形容詞　①数: many books（たくさんの本）②量: much water（たくさんの水）
2. 注意すべき名詞の数と量: My family are all fine. / There isn't much furniture in our house.

名詞の可算、不可算と関連して、物の「多い、少ない」を表す形容詞も異なってきます。また、名詞の中には数や量についてやや複雑なものもあります。「数量形容詞」と「注意すべき名詞の数と量」について、空所を埋めながら確認・整理しましょう。

1. 数量形容詞

「たくさんの～」とか「少量の～」のように、物の数や量を表す形容詞を「数量形容詞」と呼びます。代表的なものは以下の通りです。

① 数(可算名詞に): many, a lot of, lots of, some, a few, few, no

② 量(不可算名詞に): much, a lot of, lots of, some, a little, little, no

下の表は可算名詞の代表にbooksを、不可算名詞の代表にwaterを例に、数量形容詞の使われ方を示したものです。booksやwaterと一緒に発音しながら口で覚えるようにしましょう。

意　味	①数(books)	②量(water)
多い・たくさんの	many books	________ water
多い・たくさんの	a ________ of books	a lot of water
多い・たくさんの	lots of books	lots of water
いくつかの・いくらかの	some books	________ water
少数の・少量の	__________ books	____________ water
ほとんどゼロの	________ books	little water
ゼロの	no books	no water
かなり多い・たくさんの	quite a ________ books	quite a little water
少なからぬ(= たくさんの)	not a few books	not a little water

2. 注意すべき名詞の数と量

「数」や「量」の上で特に注意すべき名詞を以下に挙げます。

1) 通常、複数形で使う名詞: shoes（靴）、chopsticks（はし）、socks（靴下）など

I bought a new pair of __________ .（私は新しい靴を買いました）

2) 集合名詞

・意味によって単数または複数扱い：family（家族）, staff（スタッフ）, audience（聴衆）など

My family ________ very large.

（私の家族は大家族です）family = 1集合体 ← 単数扱い

My family ________ all fine.

（私の家族はみな元気です）family = 集合体のmembers ← 複数扱い

・常に複数扱い：police（警察）、personnel（人員）、cattle（家畜）など

The police are investigating the case.

(警察は事件を捜査している）police = police officers

3) 可算名詞のようで不可算名詞：furniture（家具）、baggage（荷物）、advice（助言）など

There isn't much furniture in our new house yet.

（私たちの新居にはまだ家具があまりない）

4) 不可算名詞の数量化

数えられない名詞も、形や器や単位によって「数える」ことができます。

a) 形を作る　　：two pieces of cake（ケーキ2個）

b) 器に入れる　：two ____________ of beer（ビール2本）

c) 単位をつける：20 grams of butter（バター 20グラム）

▶注意すべき名詞の数と量

「注意すべき名詞の数と量」についてもう少し詳しく見ていきましょう。

1）通常、複数形で使う名詞：I bought a new pair of shoes.

shoes（靴）をはじめ、chopsticks（はし）、socks（靴下）などは、いずれも「ひとつ」では使い物になりません。glasses（メガネ）、scissors（ハサミ）、jeans（ジーンズ）、pants（ズボン）なども同じです。これらは通常「一対」で使われることが多いので、例文のようにa pair of ~ を伴うことがしばしばあります。

もちろん、上記の語でも状況によっては単数形で使われることはあります。

・He dropped a chopstick.（彼ははしを1本落とした）

・A dog is holding a shoe in his mouth.（犬が靴をくわえている）

2) 集合名詞

意味によって単数または複数扱い：

・My family is very large.（family = 1集合体）

・My family are all fine.（family =集合体のmembers）

family（家族）、staff（スタッフ）、audience（聴衆）などに加え、committee（委員会）、crew（乗組員）などもこの仲間です。

・There was a large **audience** at the concert.（コンサートには大勢の聴衆がいた）

ところで、「私はグランドスタッフになりたい」は英語でどう言うでしょう？

× I want to be a ground staff.

これは誤り。「私」が「グランドスタッフという集合体」あるいは「（私1人で）グランドスタッフのmembers」になれないからです。staffの代わりにcrewを使っても同じ。正しくは、

○ I want to be a ground staff member. / I want to be a ground crew member.

3) 可算名詞のようで不可算名詞：furniture（家具）、baggage（荷物）、advice（助言）など

There isn't much **furniture** in our new house yet.

日本語で「家具」というと、テーブルやイス、ソファーなどの「（個々の）家具」を思い浮かべます。しかし、英語のfurnitureはテーブルやイスやソファーなどが集まった「家具（の集合）」を意味します。したがってwaterなどと同じ不可算名詞です。

baggageやadviceを「可算名詞」のように思うのは日本語の影響かもしれません。「荷物が2つある」とか「2、3アドバイスをいただけませんか」のように言うからです。これらも英語では不可算名詞なので two baggages とか a couple of advices などのようには言いませんので注意しましょう。

4) 不可算名詞の数量化

Grammar Review 19の2の4）以外にも不可算名詞の数量化でよく使われる表現があります。

a) 形を作る　　：two pieces of baggage（荷物2つ）、a loaf of bread（パン1斤）

b) 器に入れる　：a glass of wine（グラス1杯のワイン）、two cups of coffee（コーヒー2杯）

c) 単位をつける：three teaspoons of sugar（砂糖小さじ3杯）、50 liters of gasoline（ガソリン50リットル）

Exercises for the TOEIC® L&R Test

Part 5 Select the best answer to complete each sentence.

1. The campaign staff for the new product _______ all from the sales department.
(A) comes
(B) are
(C) is
(D) was

2. Companies invest _________ money in advertisements to attract consumers' attention.
(A) many
(B) a few of
(C) little
(D) a lot of

3. We should ask a color coordinator for _________ to make our website more attractive.
(A) an advice
(B) any advices
(C) some advices
(D) advice

4. That TV commercial is fun to watch but gives ________ information about the product.
(A) little
(B) few
(C) many
(D) any

5. The spread of the Internet has _________ influence on the way companies advertise.
(A) quite a few
(B) a lot of
(C) many
(D) a few

Part 1 Listen and select the one statement that best describes what you see in the picture. Audio② 75-77

1.

Ⓐ Ⓑ Ⓒ Ⓓ

2.

Ⓐ Ⓑ Ⓒ Ⓓ

Part 2 Listen and select the best response to each question or statement. Audio② 78-82

1. Ⓐ Ⓑ Ⓒ 2. Ⓐ Ⓑ Ⓒ 3. Ⓐ Ⓑ Ⓒ 4. Ⓐ Ⓑ Ⓒ

Part 3 Listen and select the best answer to each question. Audio② 83-85

Candidate	Gender	Age	Fee
Susie Matsumoto	Female	19	$320,000
Judy Smith	Female	28	$150,000
Betty Keaton	Female	35	$220,000
Carrie Watson	Female	42	$250,000

1. What are they talking about?
   (A) A bargain
   (B) An advertisement
   (C) A new shop
   (D) A generation gap

2. What type of company do the speakers most likely work for?
   (A) An appliance store
   (B) An automobile company
   (C) A fast-food chain restaurant
   (D) A cosmetic company

3. Look at the graphic. Which person will they most likely choose for the commercial?
   (A) Susie Matsumoto
   (B) Judy Smith
   (C) Betty Keaton
   (D) Carrie Watson

Part 4 Listen and select the best answer to each question. Audio② 86-88

SMARTPHONE	PRICE
SPW -Type A	£50
SPW -Type B	£80
SPW -Type C	£90
SPW -Type D	£120

1. How long has this store been in business?

(A) 5 years

(B) 10 years

(C) 15 years

(D) 20 years

2. What type of service is the shop offering now?

(A) Discount

(B) Free coupon

(C) Free delivery

(D) Birthday present

3. Look at the graphic. Which smartphone offers you the biggest discount?

(A) Type A

(B) Type B

(C) Type C

(D) Type D

CHAPTER 20

強調構文と倒置

At a Factory

本章での学習

▶文法：強調構文と倒置の復習・確認
▶話題：At a Factory
▶演習：Part 5 → Part 6 → Part 7形式の問題演習

事前学習

① Vocabulary 20とGrammar 20の問題に解答し、「語彙・文法クイズ」に備える。
② Part 7の英文(3つ目)をチャンク単位で全文和訳をする。

語彙・文法クイズ

Vocabulary 1 ～ 20とGrammar 1 ～ 20から5問(日本語→英語)

Vocabulary 20

Audio② 89

1 ～ 10の語句を英語にしましょう。その後で音声を聞いて確認しましょう。

1. 組み立てライン	assembly ____________
2. ～に転勤する	be ____________________ to ～
3. 注意事項	____________ & Don'ts
4. 規則を厳守する	strictly ________________ the rules
5. ～の邪魔をする	________________ with ～
6. 飲食を控える	________________ from eating and drinking
7. 本社	______________ office
8. 事業拡大	________________ expansion
9. 販売促進課	______________ Promotion Section
10. 喜んで～します。	I would be __________________ to ～.

Grammar 20

1 ～ 5の空所を埋めましょう。その後で、音声を聞いて確認しましょう。

1. 私が愛しているのはメアリーなんです。

   It is Mary ________ I love.

2. 私が彼に初めて会ったのは図書館でした。

   It was ____________________ that I first met him.

3. 彼女が初めて海外に行ったのは3年前のことでした。

   It was three years ago ________ she went abroad for the first time.

4. あなたはいったい何が言いたいのですか。

   What is ________ that you want to say?

5. 一度もないです、こんなにたくさんの星を見たことは。

   __________ have I seen so many stars.

Pair Practice

・Vocabulary 20を、瞬時に「日本語→英語」にできるように、ペア（AとB）を組んで練習しましょう（1分間）。1分後にAとBの役割を交換し、同様に練習しましょう（1分間）。

A: 教科書を見ながらBに日本語を与える

B: 教科書を閉じたままAが与える日本語を英語にする

A: Bが即答できなければ、すぐにその英語を教え、1分間の内にどの語句もスラスラ英語で言えるようにさせる

・Grammar 20の例文についても同様の練習をしましょう（1分間）。

Grammar Review 20

強調構文と倒置

1. 強調構文：It is ～ that ……（…なのは何とも～だ）
2. 倒置　　：強調語句 + 助動詞 + 何は（主語）+ どうする　…

英語で文中の一部を強調したい場合、2つの方法があります。ひとつは、It is ~ that ... という「強調構文」を使って表現する方法です。もう1つは、倒置（強調したい語句を前倒しにして置く）という手法で表現するものです。空所を埋めながら確認・整理しましょう。

1. 強調構文（It is ~ that ...）：名詞、代名詞、名詞句、名詞節、副詞句、副詞節を強調する	
作り方	普通の文の中で強調したい部分をIt is ~ that ....（…なのは何とも～だ）の～の部分に移動する。元の文で残った部分は、そのまま…の部分（thatの後）に続ければでき上がり（「もう少し詳しく」を参照）。 注意：強調される語（～の部分）が「人」の場合、thatの代わりにwhoを使うことがしばしばある。
普通の文 ↓ 強調構文	Ken saw a bear in the park last night. （ケンは昨日の夜、公園で熊を見ました） ↓　**a bear**（熊）を強調したい **It was** ＿＿＿＿＿ **that** Ken saw in the park last night. それは熊だった／ケンが昨日の夜、公園で見たのは （ケンが昨日の夜、公園で見たのは、何とも熊だった） 注意：例文のように、文の内容（…の部分）が過去の場合は、It was ~ that ...（…なのは何とも～だった）とisをwasにしてもよいし、そのままIt is ~ that ...で「…なのは～だ」としてもよい。
疑問文	**Was it** a bear **that** Ken saw in the park last night?

2. 倒置：否定の副詞（never, hardly, little, scarcely, onlyなど）を強調する	
作り方	強調したい語句を文頭に移動する。さらに、まるで疑問文のように、助動詞（助動詞、do, does, did, be動詞）を主語の前に移動し、これででき上がり（「もう少し詳しく」を参照）。
普通の文 ↓ 倒置文	I have never studied this hard in my life. （こんなに一生懸命勉強したことは自分の人生で一度もない） ↓　**never**（一度もない）を強調したい **Never** ＿＿＿＿＿ I studied this hard in my life. （一度もない／自分の人生でこんなに一生懸命勉強したことは）

▶強調構文：It is ~ that ....

この強調構文は、比較的よく使われます。理解するだけでなく、自分からも使えるように慣れ親しんでおきましょう。作り方をもう少し詳しく見ましょう。

普通の文　　Ken saw a bear in the park last night.

・a bear を強調する文　：It was a bear that Ken saw in the park last night.

同様にして

・Ken を強調する文　：It was Ken that saw a bear in the park last night.
（昨日の夜、公園で熊を見たのは、何ともケンだった）

・in the park を強調する文　：It was in the park that Ken saw a bear last night.
（ケンが昨日の夜、熊を見たのは、何とも公園でだった）

・last night を強調する文　：It was last night that Ken saw a bear in the park.
（ケンが公園で熊を見たのは、何とも昨日の夜だった）

このように、この構文は名詞（何、だれ）、代名詞、名詞句、名詞節、副詞句、副詞節（どのように、どこで、いつ、どうして）を強調するのに用います。では、残りの形容詞と動詞はどのように強調するのでしょう。

形容詞の強調： very や reallyなどを加えるだけ。
・I am happy.（私は幸せです）→ I am **very** happy.（私は幸とても幸せです）

一般動詞の強調： 現在にはdo, does, 過去にはdid を使う。
・I love you.（あなたを愛してます）→ I **do** love you.（私は本当にあなたを愛してます）
・I saw a bear.（私は熊を見ました）→ I **did** see a bear.（私は本当に熊を見たんです）

be動詞の強調： 大きな字・声で表現する。
I am happy.（私は幸せです）→ I **AM** happy.（私は本当に幸せです）

注意：「話す」ときには、当たり前のことですが、「be動詞の強調」のみならず、いずれの場合も強調する部分を強く発音することを忘れずに。

倒置による強調

前ページの表の「2. 倒置」ですが、作り方がやや複雑なので、もう少し詳しく見ていきましょう。

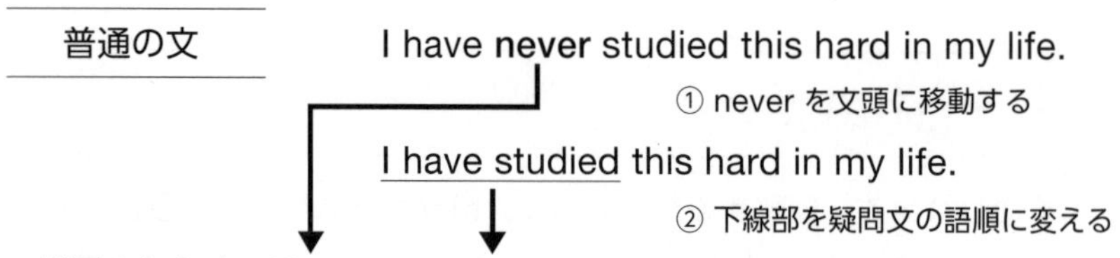

・**倒置された文：Never** have I studied this hard in my life.

Exercises for the TOEIC® L&R Test

Part 5 Select the best answer to complete each sentence.

1. It is ______ that are working on many of the assembly lines in that factory.
(A) robot
(B) a robot
(C) the robot
(D) robots

2. When was ______ that you first heard the strange noise coming from this machine?
(A) it
(B) you
(C) he
(D) she

3. ______ did I dream that I would be a factory director of such a major manufacturer.
(A) Only
(B) What
(C) Little
(D) Why

4. It was a factory in India that I was ______ to as an engineer five years ago.
(A) transferred
(B) able
(C) promoted
(D) working

5. The team leader ______ tell James to put away the tools but he forgot to do that again.
(A) will
(B) does
(C) did
(D) should

Part 6 Select the best answer to complete the text.

Dos & Don'ts on the Factory Tour

Thank you for **–1–** in this factory tour. The schedule for the day is as shown on the separate sheet. **–2–**.

PLEASE

- do not touch any machinery, equipment, products, or materials in the factory.
- do not interfere with production activities inside the factory.
- refrain **–3–** eating, drinking, and smoking inside the factory.
- **–4–** off your cell phones before entering the factory.

Should you have any questions, please ask your guide. We hope you enjoy the tour.

1. (A) participate
(B) participating
(C) to participate
(D) participated

2. (A) If you are unable to attend, please tell us as soon as possible.
(B) The factory is fully barrier-free.
(C) We ask that you strictly follow the rules below during the tour.
(D) We accept reservations up to 6 months in advance.

3. (A) from (B) by (C) of (D) to

4. (A) put (B) turn (C) call (D) take

Part 7 Read the e-mails and schedule and choose the best answer to each question.

To: All section managers
From: Peter Ward, General Affairs
Date: January 10
Subject: Opening ceremony
Attachment: Schedule

We are pleased to announce the opening of our new factory near our head office in San Diego. As you all know, it is this factory that will be a very important base for our future business expansion.

To celebrate this occasion, we are going to hold an opening ceremony. It will be in the main conference room in the new factory from 10:00 A.M. on January 30. We ask all section managers to participate.

Please see the attached sheet for the schedule for the day.

We look forward to seeing you all there.

Peter Ward
Manager, General Affairs Department

Schedule for the Opening Ceremony of Our New Factory

Time	Event	Place
09:30-10:00	Registration	Factory main entrance
10:00-10:15	Greetings: President & Plant Manager	Main conference room, 3rd floor
10:15-11:00	Factory tour	In and around the factory
11:00-12:00	Buffet party	Main cafeteria, 2nd floor

Note: If you are unable to attend or have any questions about the ceremony, please contact Jason Green of the General Affairs Department by January 15. We need catering preparations.

To: Jason Green
CC: Peter Ward
From: Becky Skinner, Sales Promotion Section
Date: January 11
Subject: Re: Opening ceremony

Thank you for the invitation to the opening ceremony of our new factory. I would be delighted to attend. However, I have a very important meeting with one of our clients at the head office at 1:00 P.M. on that day, so I have to leave the ceremony at 11:00 A.M. The meeting was scheduled a month in advance and I am giving a presentation there, so I just cannot miss it. I hope you will understand that.

Becky Skinner

1. What is the first e-mail for?
(A) Apology (B) Invitation (C) Complaint (D) Inquiry

2. How long is the whole ceremony scheduled to last?
(A) One hour (B) Two hours (C) Three hours (D) Four hours

3. Which of the following events is NOT scheduled?
(A) Speech (B) Tour (C) Party (D) Discussion

4. Why does Ms. Skinner have to leave the event early?
(A) She has to go on a business trip.
(B) She has to join a business lunch.
(C) She has to meet a client.
(D) She has to work overtime.

5. Which of the following will Ms. Skinner most likely miss?
(A) President's speech
(B) Plant Manager's speech
(C) Factory tour
(D) Buffet party

APPENDIX

重要語彙・表現リスト

Key Vocabulary

本書で扱った重要語彙のリストです。
英語 ⇄ 日本語と覚えたら、□に印を入れて予習・復習に役立てましょう。

▶Chapter 1

□ apologize for inconvenience	□ 不便を謝る
□ as a token of apology	□ お詫びの印として
□ a wide variety of vegetables	□ さまざまな種類の野菜
□ customer	□ 客
□ employment	□ 雇用
□ fill in a questionnaire	□ アンケート用紙に記入する
□ item	□ 品
□ It's amazing.	□ それはすごい。
□ renovation work	□ 改装工事
□ run a store	□ 店を経営する
□ sales assistant	□ 店員
□ temporary store	□ 一時的な店舗
□ Thank you for your patience.	□ ご迷惑をお掛けします。
□ use this app	□ このアプリを使う

▶Chapter 2

□ at the register	□ レジで
□ attract many people	□ 多くの人を引き寄せる
□ a wide variety of organic dishes	□ 多種多様なオーガニック料理
□ celebrate the opening	□ 開店を祝う
□ enclose a service coupon	□ サービス券を同封する
□ go well with the soup	□ スープに合う
□ in this neighborhood	□ この近所に
□ locally grown ingredients	□ 地元産の食材
□ menu items	□ メニューの品目
□ offer	□ 提供する
□ people concerned about calories	□ カロリーを気にしている人たち
□ reserve a seat	□ 席を予約する
□ restaurant review	□ レストランレビュー (評価)
□ the atmosphere of the restaurant	□ レストランの雰囲気
□ without worry	□ 心配せずに

▶Chapter 3

□ apply for the position	□ 求人に申し込む
□ focus on ~	□ ～に焦点を当てる
□ for security reasons	□ セキュリティー上の理由で
□ Human Resources Department	□ 人事部

□ job hunting	□ 就職活動
□ job interview	□ 就職の面接試験
□ laptop	□ ノートパソコン
□ make copies	□ コピーを取る
□ new employee	□ 新入社員
□ supervisor	□ 監督者
□ third-year student	□ 3年生
□ travel agency	□ 旅行代理店
□ use a copier	□ コピー機を使う
□ write a resume	□ 履歴書を書く

▶Chapter 4

□ achieve a goal	□ 目標を達成する
□ ask you in person	□ あなたに直接(会って)尋ねる
□ be assigned for ~	□ ～に任命される
□ be not confident in ~	□ ～に自信がない
□ colleague	□ 同僚
□ communicate with ~	□ ～とコミュニケーションを取る
□ contact ~	□ ～と連絡を取る
□ I am stuck.	□ 私は行き詰っている。
□ make full use of ~	□ ～をフル活用する
□ make yourself understood	□ 自分(あなた自身)を理解してもらう
□ manage to get through ~	□ 何とかして～を切り抜ける
□ manufacture motorcycles	□ オートバイを製造する
□ non-verbal means of communication	□ 非言語コミュニケーション手段
□ remote worker	□ リモートワーカー(遠隔勤務者)

▶Chapter 5

□ ambulance	□ 救急車
□ break down	□ 故障する
□ Can you hold on a little longer?	□ もう少し待ってもらえますか。
□ clinic	□ 診療所
□ electricity rate	□ 電気料金
□ exhibition site	□ 展示会場
□ feel sick	□ 気分が悪い
□ flow smoothly	□ スムーズに流れる
□ have it fixed	□ それを修理してもらう
□ heavy traffic on the expressway	□ 高速道路の交通渋滞
□ load the truck	□ トラックに荷物を積む
□ pick you up at the airport	□ 空港に(車で)あなたを迎えに行く
□ right away	□ すぐに
□ take three days off	□ 休暇を3日とる
□ well in advance of ~	□ ～のかなり前に

▶Chapter 6

□ audience	□ 聴衆
□ be regarded as ~	□ ～と見なされる
□ come to your mind	□ あなたの心に浮かぶ
□ definitely	□ 絶対に

- ☐ due to religious beliefs ☐ 宗教上の信仰のために
- ☐ entertain clients ☐ 顧客をもてなす
- ☐ go by myself ☐ 私一人で行く
- ☐ illegal ☐ 違法な
- ☐ Talking about ~ ☐ ～と言えば
- ☐ ten weeks in a row ☐ 10 週連続で
- ☐ theme park ☐ テーマパーク
- ☐ too scared to ~ ☐ 怖すぎて～できない
- ☐ You can't be serious. ☐ まさか本気じゃないよね（冗談だよね）。
- ☐ You must be joking. ☐ 冗談でしょう？

▶Chapter 7

- ☐ agenda ☐ 議題
- ☐ be scheduled for ~ ☐ ～に予定されている
- ☐ count on ~ ☐ ～に頼りにする
- ☐ decide the terms of the contract ☐ 契約条件を決める
- ☐ general affairs section ☐ 総務部
- ☐ lead the negotiation ☐ 交渉を主導する
- ☐ look over a schedule ☐ スケジュールに目を通す
- ☐ lower the price ☐ 価格を下げる
- ☐ office equipment ☐ オフィス用品
- ☐ personnel section ☐ 人事部
- ☐ planning section ☐ 企画部
- ☐ quote from a supplier ☐ 供給業者からの見積もり
- ☐ sales section ☐ 営業部
- ☐ server ☐ 給仕する人（ウェイター、ウェイトレス）
- ☐ teleconference ☐ テレビ会議
- ☐ tough negotiator ☐ 手ごわい交渉人

▶Chapter 8

- ☐ According to the list, … ☐ リストによると、…
- ☐ based on achievements ☐ 業績に基づいて
- ☐ discuss this matter ☐ この件について話し合う
- ☐ fireplace ☐ 暖炉
- ☐ handout ☐ 配布資料
- ☐ handout for a presentation ☐ プレゼンの配布資料
- ☐ humidifier with three functions ☐ 3機能を備えた加湿器
- ☐ make a draft ☐ 原稿を作成する
- ☐ R&D department ☐ 研究開発部
- ☐ remarkable effort ☐ 並外れた努力
- ☐ reply ASAP ☐ できるだけ早く返事をする
- ☐ sales representative ☐ 営業担当者
- ☐ significant increase ☐ 顕著な増加
- ☐ When will you be available? ☐ あなたはいつ都合がつきますか。
- ☐ work on a project ☐ プロジェクトに取り組む

▶Chapter 9

- ☐ Airbnb ☐ エアービーアンドビー（空き部屋宿泊所）
- ☐ be allowed to ~ ☐ ～することが許される

- [ ] colleague 同僚
- [ ] complaints from residents 住民からの苦情
- [ ] condominium 分譲マンション
- [ ] follow regulations 規則に従う
- [ ] garbage disposal ゴミ捨て
- [ ] ground floor 1階(主に英) = first floor (米)
- [ ] in spite of our repeated requests 再三のお願いにもかかわらず
- [ ] It's a ten-minute walk to ~ ～まで歩いて10分です。
- [ ] keep a pet in secret 秘密でペットを飼う
- [ ] nurcery school 保育園
- [ ] reserve/book a hotel room ホテルの部屋を予約する
- [ ] top priority 最優先事項
- [ ] without permission 許可なしに

▶Chapter 10

- [ ] be charged for ~ ～に対して料金を徴収される
- [ ] city hall 市役所
- [ ] due date of a book 本の返却期限
- [ ] lack of funding 資金不足
- [ ] municipal indoor swimming pool 市(自治体)の屋内プール
- [ ] parking lot 駐車場
- [ ] pay a fine of $10 10ドルの過料(罰金)を払う
- [ ] penalty 罰則
- [ ] policy on late returns 返却遅延に関する規定
- [ ] prevent heatstroke 熱中症を防ぐ
- [ ] public facilities 公共施設
- [ ] purchase price 購入価格
- [ ] renovation project 改装計画
- [ ] Thank you for your inquiry. 問い合わせありがとうございます。
- [ ] What if ... もし…だったらどうなるだろうか

▶Chapter 11

- [ ] Are you available on Friday? あなたは金曜日に都合がつきますか。
- [ ] arrange an appointment for Friday 金曜日に会うアポを設定する
- [ ] attend a meeting ミーティングに参加する
- [ ] be out of town 出張中で(こちらにはいない)
- [ ] I'm calling about ~ ～の件でお電話をしているのですが
- [ ] inform you that ... …をあなたに知らせる
- [ ] Is Friday convenient for you? 金曜日は都合がいいですか。
- [ ] Long time no see. 久しぶり。
- [ ] reschedule スケジュールを変更する
- [ ] talk to you face to face 対面であなたと話す
- [ ] talk to you in person 直接あなたと話す
- [ ] talk to you online オンラインであなたと話す
- [ ] There is no time to lose. ぐずぐずしている時間はない。

▶Chapter 12

- [ ] accept 受け入れる、承諾する
- [ ] A good idea came to my mind. いいアイディアを思いついた。

- [ ] As for ~ | ~に関しては
- [ ] attached document | 添付書類
- [ ] budget | 予算
- [ ] discuss the details | 詳細を話し合う
- [ ] feel free to ~ | 自由に（遠慮なく）~する
- [ ] if possible | もし可能であれば
- [ ] I'm tied up with ~ | 私は~で手がふさがっている
- [ ] on a regular basis | 定期的に
- [ ] project's objectives | プロジェクトの目的
- [ ] put forward suggestions | 提案を出す
- [ ] take a ten-minute break | 10分間の休憩を取る
- [ ] The sooner we meet, the better. | 会うのが早ければ早いほどよい。
- [ ] upcoming presentation | 次回のプレゼン

▶Chapter 13

- [ ] atmosphere | 雰囲気
- [ ] be involved in an accident | 事故に巻き込まれる
- [ ] be lost | 道に迷う
- [ ] business days | 営業日
- [ ] especially recommend ~ | 特に~を薦める
- [ ] fancy cafes and restaurants | しゃれたカフェやレストラン
- [ ] find an attractive shrine by chance | 偶然、魅力的な神社を見つける
- [ ] for a change | たまには気分転換に
- [ ] for a decade | 10年間
- [ ] grocery store | 食料品店
- [ ] make a discovery | 発見をする
- [ ] stall on the street | 通りの屋台
- [ ] the other day | 先日
- [ ] vegetables picked this morning | 今朝収穫された野菜

▶Chapter 14

- [ ] a fun day | 楽しい一日
- [ ] as usual | いつものように、相変わらず
- [ ] compared to last year | 去年と比べると
- [ ] go shopping downtown | 繁華街で買い物をする
- [ ] Having said that, ... | そう言ってはみたものの、…
- [ ] How about ~ing? | ~するのはどうですか。
- [ ] hug a koala | コアラを抱っこする
- [ ] I'll text you. | （携帯で）メールします。
- [ ] Not bad. | 悪くないね、いいね
- [ ] Prices are high. | 物価が高い。
- [ ] put on sunscreen | 日焼け止めを塗る
- [ ] spend all day ~ing | 一日中~して過ごす
- [ ] The flight is delayed. | 飛行機が遅れている。
- [ ] The weather has improved. | 天気が回復した。

▶Chapter 15

- [ ] boost sales | 売り上げを上げる
- [ ] call for an urgent meeting | 緊急会議を招集する

- [ ] developing countries　発展途上国
- [ ] expand a market　市場を拡大する
- [ ] He is upset.　彼は動揺している。
- [ ] heavy atmosphere　重い空気（雰囲気）
- [ ] increase sales　売り上げを増やす
- [ ] launch a new product　新製品を発売する
- [ ] on short notice　急な通知で、急遽
- [ ] overcome the worst situation　最悪の状況を乗り切る
- [ ] reflect his opinion　彼の意見を反映する
- [ ] sales target　売り上げ目標
- [ ] They are all clapping their hands.　彼らはみな拍手をしている。

▶Chapter 16

- [ ] at the latest　遅くとも
- [ ] cause you trouble　あなたに迷惑をかける
- [ ] common mistake　よくある間違い
- [ ] deal with complaints　苦情に対処する
- [ ] drinks and refreshments　飲み物と軽食（お菓子）
- [ ] explain it in detail　詳しく説明する
- [ ] in error　誤って
- [ ] lead to new business opportunities　新たな仕事の機会につながる
- [ ] new employee　新入社員
- [ ] purchase an item　品物を購入する
- [ ] shipping cost　送料
- [ ] solve the problem　問題を解決する
- [ ] Thank you for your input.　ご意見ありがとうございます。
- [ ] wrong shipment　誤配送

▶Chapter 17

- [ ] advantage of electric cars　電気自動車の利点
- [ ] electricity bill　電気料金
- [ ] endangered animals　絶滅危惧の動物
- [ ] environmental protection　環境保護
- [ ] in the long run　長い目で見ると
- [ ] It's troublesome.　それは面倒だ。
- [ ] plastic bag　ビニール袋
- [ ] plastic bottle　ペットボトル
- [ ] pollute the air　大気を汚染する
- [ ] polluted river　汚染された河川
- [ ] problems we face　私たちが直面している問題
- [ ] refrigerator　冷蔵庫
- [ ] replace it with an energy-efficient one　エネルギー効率のよいのと交換する
- [ ] serious social problem　深刻な社会問題
- [ ] use stairs instead of an elevator　エレベーターの代わりに階段を使う

▶Chapter 18

- [ ] a seven-minute walk from the station　駅から歩いて７分
- [ ] be located in ~　～に位置している
- [ ] due to my relocation　私の転勤のため

☐ floor plan of a condominium	☐ マンションの間取り
☐ housewarming party	☐ 引っ越し祝い
☐ It comes with two bedrooms.	☐ 寝室が2部屋ついています。
☐ real estate agent	☐ 不動産業者
☐ room for storage	☐ 収納スペース
☐ shuttle bus	☐ 送迎バス
☐ surrounding landscape	☐ 周囲の風景
☐ The bus leaves every 20 minutes.	☐ バスは20分ごとに出ます。
☐ The schedule is as follows.	☐ スケジュールは以下のようです。
☐ venue for a housing exhibition	☐ 住宅展示会の会場
☐ We are confident that ...	☐ …を確信しています

▶Chapter 19

☐ amazing	☐ すごい、驚きの
☐ appliance store	☐ 家電製品店
☐ appropriate	☐ 適切な
☐ ask him for advice	☐ 彼に助言を求める
☐ attract consumers' attention	☐ 客の注意を引き付ける
☐ celebrate a 10th anniversary	☐ 10周年を祝う
☐ consider a budget	☐ 予算を考慮する
☐ invest in advertisements (ads)	☐ 広告に投資する
☐ last until the end of this month	☐ 今月末まで続く
☐ lipstick	☐ 口紅
☐ offer a 30% discount	☐ 30%の割引を提供する
☐ popular sightseeing spot	☐ 人気の観光地
☐ spread of the Internet	☐ インターネットの普及
☐ target women in their 20's	☐ 20代の女性をターゲットにする
☐ walk down the stairs	☐ 階段を下りる

▶Chapter 20

☐ assembly line	☐ 組み立てライン
☐ be promoted to ~	☐ ～に昇進する
☐ be tranferred to ~	☐ ～に転勤する
☐ business expansion	☐ 事業拡大
☐ cafeteria	☐ (社員、学生)食堂
☐ Dos & Don'ts	☐ 注意事項(やっていいことと悪いこと)
☐ head office	☐ 本社
☐ I would be delighted to ~.	☐ 喜んで～します。
☐ interfere with ~	☐ ～の邪魔をする
☐ major manufacturer	☐ 大手製造業者(メーカー)
☐ put away tools	☐ 道具を片付ける
☐ refrain from eating and drinking	☐ 飲食を控える
☐ Sales Promotion Section	☐ 販売促進課
☐ strictly follow the rules	☐ 規則を厳守する

著者略歴

松岡　昇（まつおか　のぼる）

獨協大学講師、グローバル人材育成コンサルタント。
専門は国際コミュニケーション、社会言語学。『日本人は英語のここが聞き取れない』（アルク）、『会話力がアップする英語雑談 75』(DHC)、『桂三輝の英語落語』（共著、アルク）、*The Essential Guide to the TOEIC® S&W Tests*（共著、松柏社）、『公式 TOEIC® Listening & Reading 500+』（制作協力、ETS）など著書多数。大学のほか、企業のコンサルティングや研修、講演も務める。

傍島一夫（そばじま　かずお）

イギリスに語学留学後、英会話学校に就職、以降 45 年以上にわたり英語教育に携わる。
著書に *One-minute Presentation in English*（共著、松柏社）、*Beat Your Best Score on the TOEIC® L&R Test*（共著、松柏社）、*The Essential Guide to the TOEIC® S&W Tests*（共著、松柏社）など。現在は、主に企業や大学で TOEIC® L&R 対策講座やビジネスライティング講座、英会話講座など、幅広く英語研修を担当している。

▶ 写真出典
p. 109: Chapter 13-1 © www.hollandfoto.net / Shutterstock.com
p. 141: Chapter 17-2 © wjarek / Shutterstock.com

Start with Grammar Review for the TOEIC® L&R Test
文法復習型TOEIC® L&R Test対策

2023 年 4 月 5 日　初版第 1 刷発行

著　　者　松岡　昇／傍島一夫
英文校閲　Howard Colefield

発 行 者　森　信久
発 行 所　**株式会社　松 柏 社**
〒102–0072　東京都千代田区飯田橋 1 - 6 - 1
TEL 03 (3230) 4813（代表）
FAX 03 (3230) 4857
http://www.shohakusha.com
e-mail: info@shohakusha.com

装　　幀　小島トシノブ（NONdesign）
本文レイアウト・組版　株式会社インターブックス
印刷・製本　中央精版印刷株式会社
ISBN978-4-88198-784-1
略　　号 = 784